Catechism Of Karl Marx's *Capital*

A Beginner's Introduction to the Socialist Analysis of Capitalism

by Lewis Cass Fry

Red and Black Publishers, St Petersburg, Florida

First published By Economic Publishing Company, St. Louis, MO, 1905

Library of Congress Cataloging-in-Publication Data

Fry, Lewis Cass.
    Catechism of Karl Marx's Capital : a beginner's introduction to the socialist analysis of capitalism / by Lewis Cass Fry.
        p. cm.
    "First published By Economic Publishing Company, St. Louis, MO, 1905."
    ISBN 978-1-934941-99-7
1. Marx, Karl, 1818-1883. Kapital. 2. Economics. 3. Capitalism. I. Title.
    HB501.M37F8 2010
    335.4'12--dc22

                                                      2010022805

Red and Black Publishers, PO Box 7542, St Petersburg, Florida, 33734
Contact us at: info@RedandBlackPublishers.com
            Printed and manufactured in the United States of America

Contents

Preface

This great work (*Das Capital*) of Karl Marx has been before the public for years.

Its readers have mostly been scientists. And in all these years no scientist has been able to give it an adverse criticism. The subject matter is of vital importance to the general public.

Some may wonder, then, why is this work not read by the general public?

It is not strange if you take into consideration these facts.

Marx spent forty laborious years in gathering facts, he had read every author of note on political economy, from Aristotle to Herbert Spencer.

He was well versed in the philosophy of thinking and employed both the inductive and deductive methods.

He introduced the facts, classified them, according to their relations and significance, and the sequences of these facts were the premises from which he made deductions to explain individual cases.

Being of a scientific frame of mind he thought consecutively for long periods of time.

Hence the paragraphs are so long that only the best trained minds can hold a complete paragraph in consciousness, and, unless this is done the thought is not comprehended.

The work was thought out and published in German, and, although translated into English, it is still idiomatically German.

Recognizing the importance to the public weal of a clear understanding of economic problems, I concluded that the best service I could render to society was to present the contents of *Das Capital* to the public in such a manner as would be comprehensible to the most sluggish mind.

I present my efforts to the public, believing that I have, in a measure at least, solved the problem.

I force attention by a question, which compels the reader to think.

I present but a single proposition in the answer.

I make summaries which teaches the finding of relations between facts, and properly bringing them together.

Explanations are made of terms not in common use. I make digests to show what to look for in the chapter referred to.

Hoping this work will accomplish the end sought,

The Author

Part I. Commodities and Money

Chapter I. Commodities

Section 1. The two factors of a commodity: Use-value and Value. (The substance of value and the magnitude of value.)

1. The wealth of those societies in which the capitalist mode of production prevails, presents itself as an immense accumulation of commodities; its unit being a single commodity.

What presents itself? The wealth.

What wealth? The wealth of those societies in which the capitalist mode of production prevails.

How does this wealth present itself? As an immense accumulation of commodities.

What is the unit of this wealth? A single commodity.

What, then, must we begin our investigation with? The analysis of a commodity.

What do we mean by the word analysis? The separating of a thing into its elements, or parts, and considering each part separately.

2. What is a commodity? In the first place an object outside of us, a thing that by its properties satisfies human wants of some sort or another.

The nature of such wants, whether, for instance, they spring from the stomach or from fancy, makes no difference.

Neither are we here concerned how the object satisfies these wants — whether directly as a means of subsistence, or indirectly as means of production.

3. What do commodities consist of? All useful things.

How may they be looked at? From two points of view: that of quality and that of quantity.

And what are they? An assemblage of many properties.

How may they be used? In various ways.

How do we discover the various uses of things? It is the work of history.

A thing may be used today for one purpose, tomorrow for another. Hence, by all the uses it has been put to, or the history of its past uses gives us its uses of the present.

What else does this history give us? The socially recognized standard of measures for the quantity of these useful objects.

In what has the diversity of these measures origin? First, partly in the diverse nature of these objects — the liquids have gills, quarts, gallons, etc., — it would be difficult to measure liquids by the foot, yard, etc. On the other hand, it would be difficult to measure land by the quart or gallon. Second, and partly by convention.

What is here meant by "convention"? The common consent, or agreement of society.

4. What is use-value? The utility of a thing.

How is the utility of a thing limited? By its physical properties.

Has use-value any existence apart from the commodity? No.

What is a commodity as a use-value? Something useful — a utility.

A commodity, such as iron, corn, or a diamond, so far as it is a material thing, is a use-value.

Does this property — utility — depend on labor? No, it is essentially independent of the amount of labor required to appropriate its useful qualities.

What do we assume when treating of use-values? To be dealing with definite quantities — such as dozens of watches, yards of linen, tons of iron, etc.

For what special study does commodities furnish the material? That of the commercial knowledge of commodities — to be successful a merchant must know to what use a thing can be put to, in his locality.

When do use-values become a reality? Only when being consumed.

What do commodities constitute besides use-values? The substance of all wealth, whatever may be the social form of that wealth.

What are they in the society we are about to consider? The material depositories of exchange value.

What have we found, so far as we have gone in our analysis, a commodity to be? First, a material object that satisfies some human want. Second, a depository of value.

5. Our next step will be to consider exchange value.

How does exchange value first present itself? As a quantitative relation, as the proportion in which value in use of one sort, are exchanged for those of another sort.

Is this relation constant? No. The quantity of a commodity that will exchange for a certain quantity of another commodity is constantly changing with time and place.

What does exchange value appear to be? Something accidental, and purely relative, and consequently an intrinsic value.

How intrinsic? As something that is inherent in, and inseparable from commodities.

And what does this seem to be? A contradiction in terms.

Let us consider the matter a little more closely, and we will find the contradiction only seemingly so.

6. A given commodity, for example: a quarter of wheat, is exchanged for x blacking, y silk, z gold, etc., in short, for other commodities in the most different proportions.

What does x, y and z, in our illustration, mean? Quantities of an unknown amount. The quantity, whatever it may be, is represented by a letter, known quantities by the first letters, unknown quantities by the last letters of the alphabet.

What do we see by this example? First, that the wheat has many exchange values, in fact, it has as many exchange values, as there are different commodities placed in exchange with it. Second, that if x blacking, y silk, and z gold, each represent the exchange value of a quarter of wheat, they must, as exchange values be equal to each other.

What other element have we now found in a commodity? Exchange value.

What is value? Simply a mode of expression.

What does the valid exchange value of a commodity express? Something equal.

To speak proper, exchange value is value. The value of a commodity is its phenomenal form, something contained in it yet distinguishable from it.

How are the proportions in which commodities are exchangeable represented? By an equation.

7. Let us take two commodities; for example, corn and iron. The proportions in which they are exchangeable, whatever that proportion may be, can always be represented by an equation, in which a given quantity of corn is equated to some quantity of iron. For instance, 1 quarter of corn = x cwt. of iron.

What does this equation tell us? That in two different things—1 quarter of corn and x cwt. of iron—there exists in equal quantities, something common to both.

What must these two things be equal to? A third thing which, in itself, is neither the one nor the other.

What must they each, as exchange value, be reducible to? This third thing.

8. A single geometrical illustration will make this clear.

In order to calculate and compare the areas of rectilinear figures, we decompose them into triangles.

But the area of the triangle itself is expressed by something totally different from its visible figure—namely, by half the product of the base into the altitude.

Base, 6 one-half 6 = 3 x by 8 the altitude = 24 the area.

How must the exchange value of commodities be capable of being expressed? In the same way as the geometrical figure—that is, in terms of something common to them all, of which they represent a greater or less quantity.

9. Is this something common a natural property?

No. It can be neither a chemical, geometrical, nor any other natural property of a commodity—natural properties claim our attention only in so far as they affect the utility of those commodities—make them use-values.

But the exchange of commodities is evidently an act characterized by a total abstraction from its use-value. Then one use-value is just as good as another, provided only it be present in sufficient quantity. Or as old Barbon says: "One sort of wares is as good as another, if the values be equal." "There is no difference or distinction in things of equal value." "An hundred pounds' worth of lead or iron is of as great value as one hundred pounds' worth of silver or gold."

What are commodities as use-values? Above all, they are of different qualities.

What are they as exchange values? Merely different quantities, and do not contain an atom of use-value.

10. If we leave out of consideration the use-value of commodities, what have we left?

Only one common property, that of being the product of labor.

But the product of labor itself has undergone a change in our hands.

If we make abstraction from its use-value, we make abstraction, at the same time, from the material elements and shapes that make the products a use-value; we see in it no longer a table, a house, yard, or any other useful thing. Its existence as a material thing is put out of sight.

What further abstraction do we make? We make abstraction from the useful character and concrete kinds of labor embodied in the products.

And what is left? Nothing but what is common to all commodities. It is no longer the labor of the joiner, mason, tailor, spinner, nor any other concrete form of labor—all are reduced to one and the same sort of labor—human labor in the abstract.

11. Let us now consider the residue of each of these products; it consists of the same unsubstantial reality in each, a mere congealation

of homogeneous human labor, of labor power expended without regard to the mode of its expenditure.

What do these things tell us? Only that human labor power has been expended in their production, and that labor is embodied in them.

When looked at as crystals of this social substance, common to them all, what are they? Values.

12. What have we now discovered? The third thing to which the former two things are equal, which is common to them both, and is neither the one nor the other.

And that is the social substance—homogeneous human labor—i.e.,. labor in the abstract.

We also find that value expresses the quantity of homogeneous human labor embodied in a commodity. And that value manifests itself as something totally independent of the use-values, or utility of a commodity.

But if we abstract from their use-value what remains? Nothing but their value as defined above.

Therefore, the common substance that manifests itself in the exchange of commodities is their value.

The progress of our investigation will show that exchange value is the only form in which the value of commodities can manifest itself, or be expressed.

For the present, however, we have to consider the nature of value, independent of this, its form.

13. Why has an article value? Only because human labor, in the abstract, has been materialized in it.

How is the magnitude of value to be measured? Plainly, by the quantity of value creating substance—labor—contained in an article.

How is the quantity of labor measured? By its duration, labor-time finds its standard in weeks, days and hours.

14. If you shirk, or work slowly, and spend a great deal of time on the production of an article will it have more value? Indeed not. For the labor that forms the substance of value is homogeneous human labor; expenditure of one uniform labor power.

How do we determine the uniform labor power, that is, the unit of value? The total labor power of society is embodied in the sum total of the values of all commodities produced by that society, and it counts as one homogeneous mass of human labor power, although it is composed of individual units.

How do each of these individual units count when separate? The same as any other. That is, in so far as it has the character of average labor power of society, and takes effect as such. Hence, the labor power, embodied in a commodity that gives it value, is only that amount of labor-time socially necessary for its production.

How do we determine the duration of time socially necessary for the production of a given article? By that required under normal conditions of production.

What constitutes the normal condition of production? First, the degree of labor-saving machinery. Second, the average degree of skill and the intensity of labor prevalent at the time.

As an example of contrast between necessary and waste of labor-time in production we will cite: The introduction of power-looms in England, probably reduced by one-half the labor-time required to weave a given quantity of yarn into cloth.

The hand-loom weavers, as a matter of fact continued to require the same time as before.

But, for all that, the product of one hour of their labor represented, after the change, only half an hour's socially necessary labor, and consequently fell to one-half its former value.

15. What do we glean from this illustration? That which determines the magnitude of value is: the amount of labor socially necessary to produce an article.

How do we consider each individual commodity? As an average sample of its class. Commodities, therefore, in which equal quantities of labor are embodied — or which can be produced in the same time — have equal value.

What are all commodities, as values? Only definite masses of congealed labor-time.

16. Does the value of commodities remain constant? No. But it would remain constant if the labor-time required for its production remained constant.

But the labor-time changes with every variation in the productiveness of labor.

How is the productiveness of labor determined? By various circumstances, among others: First, by the average amount of skill of the workmen. Second, the state of science and the degree of its practicable application. Third, the social organization of production. Fourth, the extent and means of production. Fifth, by physical conditions.

For example: It takes the same amount of labor to plow, plant and cultivate an acre of land, one year as another. Now, if the rains, temperature and other physical conditions are favorable, the acre of land will yield, say, twenty bushels of corn. And if the climatic conditions are unfavorable it will yield, say, but ten bushels of corn.

Hence, in the unfavorable year ten bushels of corn will have embodied in them the same amount of labor as the twenty bushels of corn in the favorable year, and will, consequently, have the same value.

What appears to happen from this condition of affairs? As a large tract of land is similarly affected in the favorable year, the local market has a large supply, the unfavorable year the local market has a great demand.

What does this give rise to? The old mistaken notion that prices are regulated by the "law of supply and demand." Because in the favorable year the supply is large and prices are low. In the unfavorable year there is a seeming scarcity and prices are high.

Why is this so if "supply and demand" does not regulate prices? From the fact stated alone, in the favorable year the same labor-time, say twenty hours, is embodied in twenty bushels of corn, as in the unfavorable year in ten bushels of corn. Hence, in the favorable year corn is worth one hour's labor-time per bushel, and in the unfavorable year two hours' labor-time per bushel. Their price is governed by the law of value.

The same labor extracts from rich mines more metal than from poor ones.

Diamonds are of very rare occurrence upon the earth's surface, and hence their discovery costs, on an average, a great deal of labor-time, consequently much labor is represented in a small compass. In richer mines the same quantity of labor would embody itself in more diamonds, and their value would fall.

If we could succeed, at a small expenditure of labor, in converting carbon into diamonds, their value might fall below that of bricks.

In general, the greater the productiveness of labor, the less is the labor-time required for the production of an article, and the less is the amount of labor crystalized in that article, and the less is its value. And vice versa, the less the productiveness of labor, the greater is the labor-time required for the production of an article, and the greater is its value.

How does the value of a commodity vary? Directly, as the quantity; and inversely, as the productiveness of the labor incorporated in it.

17. Can a thing have use-value without having value? This is the case whenever its utility is not due to labor such as air, virgin soil, and natural meadows, etc.

Can a thing be useful and the product of human labor without being a commodity? Certainly! Whoever directly satisfies his wants with the produce of his own labor creates, indeed, use-values, but not commodities.

What must he do in order to create commodities? Produce use-values for others — social use-values.

Can a thing have value without having a use-value? Certainly notl If the thing is useless, so is the labor contained in it; it does not count as labor and, therefore, creates no value.

Section 2. The two-fold character of the labor embodied in commodities.

18. How did a commodity first present itself to us? As a complex thing — as use-value and exchange value.

What have we also seen concerning labor? That it, also, possesses the same two-fold nature.

How so? Because, in so far as it finds expression in value, it does not possess the same character that belongs to it, as a creator of use-values.

As a creator of value it is abstract labor, while as creator of use-values it is concrete labor.

What great importance has this feature of labor? It is the pivot on which a clear comprehension of political economy turns.

Who was the first to discover this two-fold nature of labor? Karl Marx.

Let us go more into detail and examine this two-fold character of labor.

19. Let us take two commodities, such as a coat and ten yards of linen, and let the former be double the value of the latter, so that, if ten yards of linen = W, the coat = 2 W.

20. What does the coat satisfy as a use-value? A particular want.

And to what does it owe its existence? To a special sort of productive activity.

How is its nature determined? First, by its aim. Second, by its mode of operation. Third, by its subject. Fourth, by its means. Fifth, by its result.

What do we call labor represented by the value in use of its product? Useful or concrete labor.

How do we consider it in this connection? Only by its useful effect.

21. How does the coat and linen differ? Qualitatively, as two different use-values.

How does the labor in them figure? As two different forms of useful labor — tailoring and weaving.

Why must the labor in commodities be qualitatively different? Because if the labor was not of different quality they could not stand in the relation of commodities, for one use-value is not exchanged for another of the same sort. Coats are not exchanged for coats.

22. What corresponds to all the different varieties of value in use? As many different kinds of useful labor.

How do we classify the different kinds of labor? According to the order, genus, species and variety to which they belong in the social division of labor.

NOTE — As many are not familiar with the terms used in the above paragraph I apply them to specific things:

First — Order — of industry, manufacturing, agriculture, commerce, etc.

Second — Genus — locomotive building is a genus of the order of manufacturing.

Third — Species — machinists, blacksmiths, boiler-makers, copper-smiths, molders, etc., are species of the genus locomotive building.

Fourth—Varieties—Lathe hands, planer hands, shaper hands, bolt cutters, drill press hands, etc., are varieties of the species machinist, etc. a

Is the division of labor necessary for the production of commodities? Most certainly.

Why? Because only such products can become commodities with regard to each other, as result from different kinds of labor, carried on independently and for the account of private individuals. For if all were to perform the same kind of labor there would be nothing to exchange.

Can there be a social division of labor without production of commodities? In the primitive Indian communities there is a social division of labor without the production of commodities. Their products being for use only. Today in every large factory the labor is divided according to a system, but this division is not brought about by the operatives exchanging their individual products.

23. Resume: First, in the use-value of each commodity there is contained useful labor. Second, use-values cannot confront each other as commodities unless the labor embodied in them is qualitatively different in each. Third, in a community the produce of which, in general, takes the form of commodities the qualitative difference between the useful forms of labor carried on independently by individual producers, each on his own account, develops into a complex system, a social division of labor.

What is this system called? The capitalist system of production.

24. Does it cut any figure, as regards use-value, whether the coat is worn by the tailor or his customer? None whatever, in either case it operates as a use-value.

Is the relation between the coat and the labor that produced it altered by the circumstance that tailoring has become an independent branch in the social division of labor—a special trade? Not in the least, for whenever the want of clothing forced them to it, the human race made clothes for thousands of years without a single man becoming a tailor.

To what do coats and linen owe their existence? A special productive activity, exercised with a definite aim.

What does this labor do? Appropriates particular nature-given materials to particular human wants.

What is useful labor as a creator of use-values? A necessary condition—independent of all forms of society—for the existence of the human race. It is an eternal nature imposed necessity, without which there could be no material exchange between man and nature, and therefore no life.

25. The use-values of commodities are a combination of what two elements? Matter and labor.

If we abstract the use-value from a commodity what is left? A material substratum which is not furnished by man.

NOTE —Nature alone furnishes the chemical elements—carbon, nitrogen, the alkalies, etc., that hemp absorbs from the soil in its growth. As well does nature furnish the warmth from the sun and soil that causes the capillary attraction.

How does man work? The same as nature, by changing the form of matter. And what is more, he is constantly helped by nature, in changing the form of matter.

What does this show us? That labor is not the only source of material wealth. Labor is its father and nature its mother.

26. Let us now pass from the commodity considered as a use-value to the values of commodities.

27. What did we assume? That the coat was worth twice as much as the linen. But this is a mere quantitative difference which, for the present, does not concern us.

What, then, must we bear in mind? That if the value of the coat is double that of ten yards of linen, then twenty yards of linen must have the same value as the coat.

As values, what are coat and linen? Things of a like substance— objective expressions of essentially identical labor. But tailoring and weaving are qualitatively different kinds of labor.

Are they fixed functions of different persons in all societies? No. There are states of society, in which the same man does tailoring and weaving alternately, and in this case these two forms of labor are mere modifications of the labor of the same individual. Just as the coat our tailor makes one day, and the trousers he makes another day, imply only a variation in the labor of the same individual.

How is it in our capitalist society? A given portion of human labor, in accordance with the varying demand, is at one time supplied in the form of tailoring, at another in the form of weaving. Must this change take place? Possibly not without friction, but take place it must.

NOTE—Right here our bourgeois political economists strikes a snag. "Supply and demand" receives a shock that blasts it.

A greater demand for an article causes a greater number of laborers to be employed in the production of that article.

It is a well-known fact that the greater the amount of an article produced the less labor it requires in proportion to that amount, and consequently, the less value contained in it, and the lower the price.

A greater demand always cheapens an article, providing the conditions of production remain the same.

For example—suppose you have only one coat to make, there is less labor in cutting it out with hand shears than any other way. But suppose you have 10,000 coats to make, then you can save labor by spending 490 hours in making a machine that will cut 10,000 coats per hour.

For, say, it took one hour to cut out a coat by hand, then 10,000 coats would take 10,000 hours.

Now, with the machine you could cut 10,000 coats in ten hours 490 hours' work on the machine and ten hours cutting makes 500 hours labor, this would be three minutes to each coat. Hence, each coat would contain fifty-seven minutes less time and have that amount less value in it, would be that much cheaper.

28. If we leave out of sight the special form and useful character of labor what is left? Nothing but the expenditure of human labor power, tailoring and weaving, although qualitatively different productive activities, are each a productive expenditure of human brains, nerves and muscles, and in this sense are human labor power.

What does the value of a commodity represent? Human labor in the abstract.

There are two different modes of expending labor power, of course, this labor power, which remains the same under all its modifications, must have attained a certain pitch of development before it can be expended in a multiplicity of modes.

And just as in society, a general or a banker plays a great part, but mere man, on the other hand, a very shabby part, so here with mere human labor. It is the expenditure of simple labor power, which, on an average, apart from any special development, exists in the organism of every ordinary individual.

Does this simple average labor vary? Yes, in different countries and at different times, but in a particular country it is given. How does skilled labor count? Only as simple labor intensified.

NOTE—Let us say that it takes five years to learn a particular trade, and that the average length of life in that trade is fifteen years, now, there is twenty years of labor-time spent, and necessarily so, in the articles produced during the fifteen years of skilled labor applied to the products of that artisan. Hence, three hours of his labor would be equal to four hours of simple labor.

How do we reduce the value of a commodity produced by skilled labor to the value of simple labor? By equating it to the product of unskilled labor.

How is the standard of proportion between the product of skilled and unskilled labor established? By a social process that goes on behind the backs of the producers.

How does it seem to be fixed? By custom. Hence for simplicity's sake, we will count every kind of labor to be unskilled, simple labor. By this we do more than save ourselves the trouble of making the reduction.

29. What do we do in viewing the coat and linen as values? Abstract from their different use-values.

How do we treat the labor representing those values? We disregard the difference between its useful forms—tailoring and weaving.

What are coat and linen as use-values? Special productivities with cloth and yarn.

What are they as values? Mere homogeneous congealations of undifferentiated human labor.

How does the labor embodied in these values count? Only as the expenditure of human labor power, and not by its productive relation with cloth and yarn.

Why are tailoring and weaving necessary factors in the creation of use-values, coat and linen? Because these two kinds of labor are of different qualities.

How is it that they both form the substance of the values of the same articles? Only in so far as abstraction is made from their special qualities, and that both possess the quality of being human labor.

30. What are coat and linen more than values? Values of definite quantities.

What have we assumed? That the coat is worth twice as much as ten yards of linen.

Whence this difference in their values? Because, in the production of the coat labor-time must have been expended during twice the time necessary for the production of ten yards of linen.

31. How does labor count with reference to use-value? Qualitatively.

How does labor count with reference to value? Quantitatively.

What must the labor as value be reduced to? Human labor pure and simple.

In the former case it is a question of how and what?

In the latter of how much? How long a time?

Since the magnitude of the value of a commodity represents only the quantity of labor embodied in it, what follows? That all commodities when taken in certain proportions are equal in value.

32. If the productive power of all sorts of labor remains the same, how could the value of coats be increased? Only by the increase of the number of coats. If one coat represents one day's labor, two coats would represent two days' labor, and so on for the number of coats produced.

Assume the labor-time necessary to produce a coat become doubled, then what? One coat is worth as much as two coats were before.

Assume the labor-time necessary to produce a coat be reduced by one-half, what then? Two coats are worth only as much as one was before.

Does either of these changes alter, in any way, the use-value of coats? Not in the least, for the coat renders the same service as before, and the labor embodied in coats remain of the same quality, but the quantity of labor spent on coats has altered.

33. What does an increase of use-value give us? An increase of material wealth. With two coats two men can be clothed, while with one coat only one man can be clothed.

Does an increase of wealth always give us an increase of value? No. For we may have an increase of wealth and a decrease of the magnitude of value at the same time.

In what has this antagonistic movement its origin? In the twofold character of labor.

To what have we reference when we say the productive power of labor? Only of labor of some useful concrete kind.

Upon what does the efficacy of any special productivity during a given time depend? Its productiveness.

What does useful labor become? A more or less abundant source of products, in proportion to the rise or fall of its productiveness.

Does the change in productiveness affect the labor represented by value? No. For so soon as we make abstractions from the concrete useful forms it can no longer have any bearing on that labor.

However then, however productive power may vary, the same labor, exercised during equal periods of time always yield equal amounts of value.

The same change in productive power, which increases the fruitfulness of labor, and, in consequence, the quantity of use-values produced by that labor will diminish the total value of this increased use-values, provided such change shorten the total labor-time necessary for their production and vice versa.

34. On the one hand, all labor is, speaking physiologically, an expenditure of human labor-power, and in its character of identical abstract human labor it creates and forms the value of commodities.

On the other hand, all labor is the expenditure of human labor-power in a special form and with a definite aim; and, in this, its character of concrete useful labor, it produces use-values.

Section 3. — The Form of Value, or Exchange Value.
35. How do commodities come into the world? In the shape of use-values, articles or goods, such as iron, linen, corn, etc., this is their plain, homely, bodily form.

Why are they commodities? Only because they are something, two-fold — both objects of utility, and at the same time depositories of value.

How do they manifest themselves as, or have the form of, commodities? Only in so far as they have two forms — a physical or material form, and a value-form.

36. Is the value of a commodity a material substance? No, indeed, not an atom of the material substance of a commodity enters into its value.

Examine a single commodity as you will and in so far as it remains an object of value it seems impossible to grasp it.

What must we bear in mind to comprehend the value of a commodity? That it has a purely social reality.

How is this reality acquired? Only in so far as they are expressions or embodiments of one identical social substance—namely, human labor.

And it follows, as a matter of course, that value can manifest itself only in the social relation of commodity to commodity.

Where did we start from? Exchange value, or the exchange relation of commodities.

And what have we found? The value that lies hidden behind it.

37. We must now return to this form under which value first appeared to us.

Everyone knows, if he knows nothing else, that commodities have a value form common to them all, and present a marked contrast with the varied bodily forms of their use values.

What is this value form of commodities? The money form.

What task have we now before us? One that no bourgeois economist has ever attempted to perform.

And what is that? Tracing the genesis of the money form, or developing the expression of value implied in the value relation of commodities, from its simplest, almost imperceptible outline to the dazzling money form.

What do we accomplish, at the same time, by doing this? Solve the great sphinx-like riddle presented by money.

38. What is the simplest value relation? That of one commodity to some one other commodity of a different kind.

What does the value relation between two commodities supply us with? The simplest expression of the value of a single commodity; and gives us the elementary form of value.

A.—Elementary or accidental form of value.

X com. A = Y com. B. or X com. A. is worth Y com. B.

Twenty yards of linen = 1 coat, or 20 yards of linen are worth 1 coat.

l. The two poles of the expression of value; relative form and equivalent form.

The whole mystery of the form of value lies hidden in this elementary form. Its analysis, therefore, is our real difficulty.

39. What are the parts played by the two different commodities? One, the linen, plays an active part, it expresses its value in the coat. The other, the coat, plays a passive part, it serves as the material in which value is expressed.

How is the linen represented? As relative value, or it appears in relative form.

How does the coat officiate? As equivalent, or appears in equivalent form.

40. How are these two forms considered? As poles of the same expression.

They are two intimately connected, mutually dependent, and inseparable elements of the expression of value; but at the same time, mutually exclusive and antagonistic extremes. Hence, poles that are as opposites, as the poles of a magnet.

How are they alloted? Respectively to the two different commodities brought into relation by that expression.

Twenty yards of linen = twenty yards of linen is no expression of value.

It simply says that twenty yards of linen is twenty yards of linen — a definite quantity of linen.

How can the value of the linen be expressed? Only relatively, that is, in some other commodity.

What does the relative form of the value of the linen presuppose? The presence of some other commodity in the form of equivalent — in this case the coat.

Can the equivalent commodity, at the same time, assume the relative form? No, indeed.

What is its function? To serve as the material for expressing the value of other commodities.

41. What does the expression twenty yards of linen = one coat imply? The opposite relation, one coat = twenty yards of linen.

What would the reversed equation, one coat = twenty yards of linen, express? The relative value of the coat.

What does the linen become? The equivalent instead of the coat.

A single commodity cannot, therefore, simultaneously assume, in the same expression of value, both forms.

The very polarity of these forms makes them mutually exclusive.

42. Upon what does it depend, which form of value a commodity assumes? Entirely upon accident, that is, whether it is the one expressing value, or the one whose value is being expressed.

2. *The relative form of value.*

A. The nature and import of this form.

43. How can we discover how the elementary expression of the value of a commodity lies hidden in the value relation of two commodities? By considering the value relation of the two commodities entirely apart from their quantative aspect.

What is the usual mode of procedure? Generally the reverse, and in the value relation nothing is seen, but the proportions between definite quantities of two different sorts of commodities, that are considered equal to each other.

What, then, is apt to be forgotten? That the magnitude of different things can be compared, quantitatively, only when those magnitudes are expressed in terms of the same unit. It is only as expressions of such a unit that they are of the same denomination and, therefore, commensurable.

44. What is the basis of our equation? Linen = coat.

What does it imply whether twenty yards of linen = one coat or = two coats, or = x coats, that is, whether a given quantity of linen is worth few or many coats? That linen and coats as magnitudes of value, are expressions of the same unit, things of the same kind. Linen and coat is the basis of the equation.

45. But the two commodities whose identity of quality is thus assumed do not play the same part.

What is expressed? Only the value of the linen.

How? By its reference to the coat as its equivalent, as something that can be exchanged for it.

What is the coat, in this relation, as equivalent? The mode of existence of value, value embodied; for only as such is it the same as the linen.

Why does the linen's own value come to the front and receive independent expression? Only because that it is value, is it comparable with the coat as a thing of equal value, or exchangeable with it. To make this more clear, let us borrow an illustration from chemistry. In chemistry there are two substances that are compounds of the same chemical substances. One is butyric acid, the other is propyle formate. They are not only of the same chemical substance, but are also of the same proportion of each. Namely, butyric acid consists of carbon, 4, hydrogen, 8, and oxygen, 2; propyle formate also consists of carbon, 4; hydrogen, 8, and oxygen, 2. Now, if we equate butyric acid to propyle formate, then, in the first place, propyle formate would be, in this relation, merely a form of existence of carbon, 4; hydrogen, 8; oxygen, 2 parts. Next we would be stating that butyric acid also consists of carbon, 4; hydrogen, 8, and oxygen, 2.

Thus by equating the two substances, expression would be given to their chemical composition, while their different physical forms would be neglected.

46. Now, in our consideration of commodities we have noticed only the relation of value.

What do we reduce commodities to when we say that they are only the congealation of human labor? To the abstraction — value.

Do we ascribe to this value any particular form? None apart from their bodily form.

How is it when we place commodities in value relation with one another? Then one stands forth in its character of value, by reason of its relation to the other.

47. What have done in making the coat equivalent to the linen? Equated the labor embodied in the coat to the labor embodied in the linen, although tailoring, which makes the coat is concrete labor, of a different sort from the weaving that makes the linen.

What reduces these different kinds of labor to their common character, that of human labor? The act of equating the different commodities.

What does this express? The fact that weaving—in so far as it weaves values, has nothing to distinguish it from tailoring, and, consequently, is abstract human labor.

What brings into relief the specific character of value-creating labor? The expression of equivalence between different sorts of commodities, by actually reducing the labor embodied in them to its common quality of human labor in the abstract.

48. What is required beyond the expression of the specific character of labor, which is value? It must have objective existence. That is it must be embodied in some object.

Is human labor-power, in itself, value? No, indeed.

How does labor become value? Only by being congealed—that is, when embodied in some object.

How must the value of a commodity be expressed? As something materially different from the commodity, and yet as something common to it, and to all other commodities. The problem is already solved.

49. How does the coat rank qualitative as the equal of the linen? As something of the same kind, because it is value.

How do we see the coat, when in the position of equivalent? As nothing but value, a something whose palpable bodily form represents value.

What is the body of the commodity—coat—itself? A mere use-value. And as a coat, it no more tells that it is value than the first piece of linen we take hold of.

What does this show us? That when put in value relation the coat has more signication than when out of that relation.

50. How is the coat a depository of value? In the production of the coat, human labor-power, in the shape of tailoring must have been actually expended. Human labor-power is, therefore, accumulated in it. And in this aspect the coat is a depository of value. But though worn to a thread it does not let this fact show through.

How does the coat exist, as equivalent to the linen, in the value equation? As a depository of value—as embodied value—as a body that is value.

A, for instance, cannot be "your majesty" to B, unless at the same time majesty in B's eyes assumes the bodily form of A, and, what is more, with every new father of the people, changes its features, hair, and many other things besides.

51. How does the coat, as equivalent of the linen, officiate in the value equation? As the form of value. The value of the linen is expressed by the bodily form of the coat, that is, by the use-value coat.

As use-value, are coat and linen the same? No, they are palpably different. But, as values, they are the same, and, furthermore, the linen has the same appearance as the coat. Thus the linen acquires a value-form different from its physical form.

The fact that it is value is made manifest by its equality with the coat. Just as the sheep's nature of a Christian is shown in his resemblance to the Lamb of God.

52. We see, then, all that our analysis of a commodity has already told us, is told us by the linen itself, so soon as it comes into communication with another commodity — the coat. Only it betrays its thoughts in the language with which it is familiar, the language of commodities.

In order to tell us that its own value is created by labor, in its abstract character of human labor, it says that the coat, in so far as it is worth as much as the linen, and therefore is value, consists of the same labor as the linen.

In order to inform us that its sublime reality as value is not the same as its buckram body, it says that value has the appearance of a coat, and, consequently, that so far as the linen is value, it and the coat are like as two peas.

53. Summary — By means, therefore, of the value relation expressed in our equation, the bodily form of commodity B becomes the value form of commodity A, or the body of commodity B acts as a mirror to the value of commodity A.

NOTE — In a sort of way it is with man as it is with commodities: Since he comes into world neither with a looking glass in his hand nor as a Fichtian philosopher, to whom "I am I" is sufficient. Man first sees and recognizes himself in other men. Peter only establishes his own identity as a man by first comparing himself with Paul as being of like kind. And thereby Paul, just as he stands in his Pauline personality, becomes to Peter the type of the genus, Homo.

By putting itself in relation with commodity B, as value in propria persona, as the matter of which human labor is made up, the commodity A converts the value in use, B, into the substance in which to express its, A's own value. The value of A thus expressed in the use-value of B has taken the form of relative value.

2. Quantitative determination of relative value.

54. What is every commodity, whose value it is intended to express? A useful object of given quantity, such as 15 bushels of corn, or 100 pounds of coffee.

What does a given quantity of any commodity contain? A definite quantity of human labor.

What must the value form express, besides value in general? Value of a definite quantity. Therefore, in the value relation of commodity A (linen) to commodity B (coat), not only is the coat, as value in general, made the equal in quality of the linen, but a definite quantity of coat (one coat) is made the equivalent of a definite quantity (twenty yards) of linen.

What does the equation, twenty yards of linen = one coat imply? That the same quantity of value substance (congealed labor) is embodied in both; that the two commodities have cost the same amount of labor-time.

As the labor-time necessary for the production of twenty yards of linen, or one coat varies with every change in the productiveness of tailoring and weaving what must we consider? The influence of such change on the quantitative aspect of the relative expression of value.

56. Let the value of the linen vary, in magnitude, the coat remaining the same.

If in consequence — of the exhaustion of flax-growing soil, or from any other cause, the labor-time necessary for the production of the linen be doubled, how would it effect the relative Value of the linen? It would be doubled.

How would the equation stand? Twenty yards of linen = two coats. Why? Because, now, one coat contains only half the labor-time embodied in twenty yards of linen.

On the other hand, if in consequence of improved looms, or from any other cause, the labor-time necessary to produce twenty yards of linen fall by one-half, how would it affect the relative value of the linen? It would fall by one-half, consequently we would have twenty yards of linen = one-half coat. From this we deduce Rule I. The relative value of A (linen) expressed in commodity B (coat) rises and falls directly as the value of A (linen). The value of B (coat) remaining the same.

57. Now let the value of the linen remain constant, while the value of the coat varies in magnitude.

If, from any cause, the labor-time necessary for the production of the coat be doubled, what is the equation? Twenty yards of linen equal one-half coat.

If the value of the coat sinks by one-half what is the equation? Twenty yards of linen equal two coats.

From this we deduce Rule II. The value of commodity A (linen) remaining constant, its relative value expressed in commodity B (coat) rises and falls inversely as the value of B (coat).

58. What do we find by comparing the different in cases Rules I and II? That the same change of magnitude in relative value may arise from totally opposite causes. Thus the equation twenty yards of linen equal one coat, becomes twenty yards of linen equal two coats, either, because the value of the linen has doubled, or because the value of the coat has fallen by one-half. On the other hand it becomes twenty yards of linen equal one-half coat, either because the value of the linen has fallen by one-half, or because the value of the coat has doubled.

59. Let the quantity of labor-time necessary for the production of linen and coat vary simultaneously in the same direction and in the same proportion, what would the equation be? The same—twenty yards of linen equal one coat—however much their values may have altered.

Then how do we find out that their values has changed? By comparing them to a third commodity whose value has remained constant. Rule III.

But suppose that the values of all commodities rose or fell simultaneously. Then how could we tell that their values had changed, their relative value being unaltered? Their real change of value would appear from the diminished or increased quantities of commodities produced in a given time.

60. The labor-time respectively necessary for the production of the linen and coat, and therefore, the value of these commodities, may simultaneously vary in the same direction, but at unequal rates, or in opposite direction, or in other ways.

The effect of all these possible different variations, on the relative value of a commodity, may be deduced from the results of Rules I, II and III.

61. Summary — The real changes in the magnitude of value are neither unequivocally nor exhaustively reflected in their relative expression, that is, in the equation expressing the magnitude of relative value.

The relative value of a commodity may vary, although its real value remains constant.

Its relative value may remain constant although its value varies. And, finally, simultaneous variations in the magnitude of value and in that of its relative expression by no means correspond in amount.

3. The equivalent form of value.

62. How does a commodity, coat, become impressed with a specific value form, namely, the equivalent form? Simply by a commodity of a different kind — linen — expressing its value in the use-value of that commodity — coat.

How does the commodity linen manifest its quality of having value? By the fact that the coat, without having assumed a value form different from its bodily form, is equated to the linen.

How is the fact, that the coat has value, expressed? By saying that the coat is directly exchangeable with the linen.

What do we express by saying a commodity has the equivalent form? That it is directly exchangeable with other commodities.

63. When one commodity, such as a coat, serves as the equivalent of another, such as linen, and coats consequently acquire the characteristic property of being directly exchangeable with linen, we are far from knowing in what proportion the two are exchangeable.

Upon what does the proportion depend, the value of the linen being given in magnitude? On the value of the coat.

How is the magnitude of the coat's value determined? Entirely independent of its value form, by the labor-time necessary for its production.

How does the coat, in the equation of value, as the equivalent, figure? Only as a definite quantity of some article.

64. For instance, forty yards of linen are worth — what? Two coats.

Why? Because the coat here plays the part of equivalent. Because the use-value, coat, as opposed to the linen, figures as an embodiment of value. Hence, a definite number of coats suffices to express a definite quantity of linen.

What may express the value of forty yards of linen? Two coats.

Can the two coats express their own value? Never!

A superficial observation of this fact, namely, that in the equation of value, the equivalent figures exclusively as a simple quantity of some article, of some use-value, has mislead Bailey, as well as some others, both before and after him, into seeing, in the expression of value, merely a quantitative relation; the truth being that, when a commodity acts as an equivalent no quantitative determination is expressed.

65. What is the first peculiarity that strikes us in considering the form of the equivalent? That use-value becomes the form of manifestation of the phenomenal form — its opposite — value.

66. When does the bodily form of a commodity become its value form? Only when some other commodity enters into a value relation with it, and then only within that relation. Since no commodity can stand in relation of equivalent to itself, and thus turn its own bodily shape into the expression of its own value, every commodity is compelled to choose some other commodity for its equivalent and to accept the use-value — that is to say the bodily shape — of that commodity as the form of its own value.

67. One of the measures that we apply to commodities as material substance — as use-value — will serve to illustrate this point.

A sugar-loaf being a body, is heavy, and therefore has weight; but we can neither see nor touch this weight. We then take various pieces of iron, whose weight has been determined before hand. The iron, as iron, is no more the manifestation of weight than is the sugar-loaf.

How do we express the sugar-loaf as so much weight? We put it in weight relation with the iron.

How does the iron officiate in this relation? As a body representing nothing but weight.

How does the iron express the weight of the sugar-loaf? A certain quantity of iron serves as the measure of the weight of the sugar, and represents, in relation to the sugar-loaf, weight embodied, and is the form or manifestation of weight.

When does the iron manifest weight? Only when the body whose weight has to be determined enters into weight relation with the iron.

Why are they capable of entering into this relation? Because they are both heavy. Were they not both heavy they could not enter into this relation, and the one could not serve as the expression of the weight of the other.

What do we find when both are thrown into the scales? That in reality, as weight, both are the same; and, that when taken in the proper proportions, they have the same weight. Just as the substance iron, as a measure of weight, represents in relation to the sugar-loaf, weight alone. So, in our expression of value, the material object coat, in relation to linen, represents value alone.

68. Here, however, our analogy ceases, and why? Because the iron, in the expression of the weight of the sugar-loaf represents a natural property common to both bodies—namely, their weight.

While the coat, in the expression of the value of the linen, represents a non-natural property of both, something purely social—namely, their value.

69. How do we discover that a social relation lies at the bottom of the relative value form? Since the relative value form of a commodity—the linen for example—expresses the value of that commodity as being something wholly different from its substance and properties, as being, for instance, coat-like, we see that this expression itself indicates that some social relation lies at the bottom of it.

How is it with the equivalent form? Just the contrary. For the very essence of this form is that the material substance itself—the coat, just as it is—expresses value, and is endowed with the form of value by nature herself.

Does this hold good under all circumstances? No. This holds good only so long as the value relation exists, in which the coat stands in the position of equivalent to the linen.

Is the property of a thing the result of its relation to other things? Certainly not; but only manifest themselves in such relation.

How do they seem when in such relation? The coat seems to be endowed with the equivalent form—its property of being exchangeable—just as much by nature as it is endowed with the property of being heavy, or the capacity to keep us warm. Hence the enigmatical character of the equivalent form escapes the notice of the bourgeois political economist until this form, completely developed, confronts him in the shape of money.

Then how does he seek to explain away the mystical character of gold and silver? By substituting for them less dazzling commodities, and, by reciting, with ever-renewed satisfaction the catalogue of all possible commodities which, at one time or another, played the part of equivalent.

He has not the least suspicion that the most simple expression of value, such as twenty yards of linen equal one coat, already propounds the riddle of the equivalent for our solution.

70. The body of the commodity that serves as equivalent figures as the materialization of human labor in the abstract. And yet what is it? The product of some specifically concrete labor.

What does this concrete labor become? The medium for expressing abstract human labor.

While the coat ranks as nothing but the embodiment of abstract human labor, how does the specific labor of tailoring count? As nothing but the form, under which that abstract labor is realized.

Of what does tailoring, in the expression of the value of the linen, consist? Not in making clothes, but in making an object which we at once recognize to be value, and therefore to be a congealation of labor.

But, of what kind of labor? Labor indistinguishable from that realized in the linen.

What must the labor of tailoring reflect, to act as a mirror of value to the linen? Nothing but its own abstract quality of being human labor generally.

71. In tailoring, as well as weaving, human labor-power is expended.

How must they be considered, in the production of value? Under the aspect, of both possessing the general property of being human labor, and under this aspect alone.

But how is the fact to be expressed, that weaving creates the value of the linen—not by being weaving, as such—but by its general property of being human labor? Simply by opposing to weaving, that other form of concrete labor—tailoring—which produces the equivalent of the product of weaving.

Just as the coat in its bodily form became a direct expression of value, so now does tailoring, a concrete form of labor, appear as the direct and palpable embodiment of human labor generally.

72. What is the second peculiarity of the equivalent form? That concrete labor becomes the form under which its opposite, abstract labor, manifests itself.

73. Why does this concrete labor, tailoring, rank identical with the weaving embodied in the linen? Because it is identical with undifferentiated labor, therefore, ranks identical with any other sort of labor.

What is all commodity producing labor? The labor of private individuals.

How does it rank? As labor directly social in its character. And this is the reason why the product of tailoring is exchangeable with all other commodities.

What is the third peculiarity of the equivalent form? That the labor of private individuals takes the form of its opposite, labor directly social in its form.

74. The two latter peculiarities of the equivalent form will become more intelligible if we go back to the great thinker, who was the first to analyze so many forms, whether of thought, society or nature, and among them also the form of value. I mean Aristotle.

75. In the first place he clearly enunciated that the money form of commodities is only the further development of the simple form of value—that is the expression of the value of one commodity in some other commodity taken at random—for, he says: "Five beds equal one house is not to be distinguished from five beds equal so much money."

76. He further sees that the value relation which gives rise to this expression makes it necessary that the house should qualitatively be

made the equal of the bed, and, that without such an equation, these two clearly different things could not be compared with each other as commensurable quantities.

"Exchange," he says, "cannot take place without equality, and equality not without commensurability."

Here, however, he comes to a stop and gives up the further analysis of the form of value.

"It is, however, in reality, impossible that such unlike things can be commensurable—that is, qualitatively equal."

"Such an equalization can only be something foreign to their real nature, consequently, a make-shift for practical purposes."

77. Aristotle, therefore, himself tells what barred the way to his further analysis.

It was the absence of any concept of value.

What is that equal something, that common substance, which admits of the value of the beds being expressed by the house? Such a thing, in truth, cannot exist. And why not? Compared with the beds, the house does represent something equal to them, really equal both in the beds and in the house, and that is human labor.

78. What prevented Aristotle from seeing the important fact that, to attribute values to commodities, is merely expressing all labor as equal human labor? This: Greek society was founded upon slavery and had, therefore, for its natural basis the inequality of men and of their labor powers.

What is the secret of the expression of value? That all kinds of labor are equal and equivalent, because, and in so far, as they are human labor in general.

What are the conditions under which we are able to decipher this secret? That the notion of human equality has acquired a fixed popular prejudice.

And in what society can such a prejudice be prevalent? Only in such societies, as in which the produce of labor takes the form of commodities, in which, consequently, the dominant relation between man and man is that of owners of commodities.

In other words, only in capitalist societies.

The brilliancy of Aristotle's genus is shown by this alone, that he discovered, in the expression of the values of commodities, a relation of equality.

The peculiar condition of the society in which he lived alone prevented him from discovering what "in truth" was at the bottom of this equality.

The elementary form of value considered as a whole.

79. In what is the elementary form of the value of a commodity contained? The equation, expressing the value relation of one commodity to another of a different kind — or its exchange relation to the same.

How is the value of a commodity qualitatively expressed? By the fact that other commodities are directly exchangeable with it.

How is the value of a commodity quantitatively expressed? By the fact that a definite quantity of B (coat) is exchangeable with a definite quantity of A (linen).

In other words, the value of a commodity obtains independent and definite expression, by taking the form of exchange value.

When, at the beginning of this chapter, we said, in common parlance, that a commodity is both a use-value and an exchange value, we were, accurately speaking, wrong.

A commodity is a use-value, or object of utility, and a value.

When does a commodity manifest itself as this two-fold thing? As soon as its value assumes an independent form — namely, the form of exchange value.

It never assumes this form when isolated, but only when put in a value, or exchange, relation with another commodity of a different kind; when once we know this, such a mode of expression, as use value and exchange value, does no harm, it simply serves as an abbreviation.

80. What has our analysis shown, as regards the origin of the expression of value? That the form, or the expression, of the value of commodities originate in the nature of value, and not that value originates in the mode of their expression as exchange value.

That value and its magnitude originate in their mode of expression, is the delusion, as well of the mercantilist and their recent revivers, Ferreir, Ganihl and others, as also of their antipodes, the modern bagmen of Free Trade, such as Bastiat.

The mercantilist lay special stress on the qualitative aspect of the expression of value, and consequently on the equivalent form of commodities, which attains its full perfection in money. The modern hawkers of Free Trade, who must get rid of their article at any price, on the other hand, lay most stress on the quantitative aspect of the relative form of value.

For them, consequently, there exists neither value nor magnitude of value, anywhere except in its expression by means of the exchange relation of commodities—that is, in the daily lists of prices current.

MacLeod, who has taken upon himself to dress up the confused ideas of Lombard Street in the most learned finery, is a successful cross between the superstitious mercantilist and the enlightened Free Trade bagmen.

81. A close scrutiny of the expression of the value of A (linen) in terms of B (coat) contained in the equation expressing the value relation of A to B has shown us, that, within that relation, the bodily form of A figures only as use-value, the bodily form of B only as the form or aspect of value.

The opposition or contrast, existing internally in each commodity between use-value and value is, therefore, made evident externally by the two commodities being placed in such relation to each other that the commodity whose value it is sought to express figures directly as use-value, while the commodity in which that value is to be expressed figures directly as mere exchange value.

Hence the elementary form of value of a commodity is the elementary form in which the contrast contained in that commodity, between use-value and value becomes apparent.

82. What is every product of labor, in every state of society? A use-value.

When does the product of labor become a commodity? Only at a definite historical epoch in a society's development, namely, at that epoch when the labor spent on the production of a useful article becomes expressed as one of the objective qualities of that article—that is its value.

What does this show us? That the elementary form is also the primitive form under which the product of labor appears historically as a commodity.

And, that the gradual transformation of such products proceed step by step with the development of the value form.

83. What do we now perceive, at first sight? The deficiency of the elementary form of value.

What must it undergo before it can ripen into the price form? A series of metamorphoses — changes.

84. What does the expression of the value of commodity A, in terms of another commodity B, distinguish? The value from the use-value of A.

How does it place A? Merely in a relation of exchange with a single different commodity B.

But it is still far from expressing A's qualitative equality, and quantitative proportionality, to all other commodities.

What corresponds to the elementary relative value form of a commodity? Only the single equivalent form of one other commodity.

Thus in the relative expression of value of the linen, the coat assumes the form of equivalent, or of being directly exchangeable only in relation to a single commodity, the linen.

85. What action does the elementary value form take? It passes, by an easy transition, into a more complete form.

It is true that, by means of the elementary form, the value of a commodity A, becomes expressed in terms of one, and only one, other commodity.

But what might that commodity be? A commodity of any kind, coat, iron, corn, or anything else.

As we place A in relation with one or the other of these commodities what do we get? Different elementary expressions of value for the same commodity.

How are the number of such possible expressions limited? Only by the number of different kinds of commodities distinct from it.

What does this convert the isolated expressions of A's value into? A series, prolonged to any length, of the different elementary expressions of that value.

B. *Total or expanded form of value.*

Twenty yards of linen = 1 coat or = 10 pounds of tea or = 40 pounds of coffee or = 1 quarter of corn or = 2 ounces of gold or= 1-2 ton of iron or = etc.

1. – *The expanded relative form of value.*

86. How is the value of a single commodity, linen for example, now expressed? In terms of numberless other elements of the world of commodities.

And what does every other commodity become? The mirror of the linen's value.

It is thus, for the first time, that this value shows itself in its true light, as a congealation of undifferentiated labor.

How does the labor embodied in the linen, now, stand? Expressly revealed as labor that ranks equally with every other sort of human labor, no matter what its form, whether tailoring, plowing, mining, etc., and no matter, therefore, whether it is realized in coats, corn, iron, or gold.

How does the linen, by virtue of its value form, now, stand? In a social relation, no longer with only one other kind of a commodity, but with the whole world of commodities.

As a commodity it is a citizen of the world.

What does this interminable series of equations imply? That, as regards the value of a commodity, it is a matter of indifference under what particular form, or kind of use-value it appears.

87. Does our first form, 20 yards of linen = 1 coat, assure us that commodities are exchangeable in definite quantities? Not at all, for aught that otherwise appears, it might be purely accidental that these two commodities are exchangeable in definite quantities.

Where do we at once, perceive the background that determines, and is essentially different from, this accidental appearance? In the second form — B.

How so? Because the value of linen remains unaltered in magnitude, whether expressed in coats, coffee, iron, or in numberless different commodities, the property of as many different owners.

What, now, becomes plain? That it is not the exchange of commodities that regulates their exchange value, but, on the contrary, it is the magnitude of their value that controls their exchange proportions.

2. The particular equivalent form.

88. How does each commodity now figure? A commodity, such as coat, tea, corn, iron, etc., figures in the expression of value of the linen, as an equivalent, and, consequently, as a thing that is value. How

does the bodily form of these commodities figure? As a particular equivalent form, one out of many.

How does the manifold useful kinds of labor, embodied in these communities, rank? As so many forms of the realization, or manifestations, of undifferentiated human labor.

3. Defects of the total or expanded form of value.

89. Why is the relative expression of value incomplete, in the expanded form? Because the series representing it is interminable.

How so? Because, in the first place, the chain of which this equation is but a link, is liable, at any moment, to be lengthened by each new kind of commodity that comes into existence and furnishes the material for a fresh expression of value.

And, in the second place, it is a many-colored mosaic of disparate and independent expressions of value.

And, lastly, if, as must be the case, the relative value of each commodity in turn becomes expressed in this expanded form, we get for each of them a relative value form, differing in each case, and consisting of an interminable series of expressions of value.

How are the defects of the expanded relative value-form reflected? In the corresponding equivalent form.

Since the bodily form of each single commodity is one particular equivalent form among numberless others, what have we? Nothing but fragmentary equivalent forms excluding each other.

How is the special concrete, useful kinds of, labor embodied in each particular equivalent presented? Only as a particular kind of labor, therefore not as an exhaustive representative of human labor generally.

How does human labor generally gain adequate manifestation? In the totality of its manifold, particular, concrete forms.

But, in that case, its expression in an infinite series is ever incomplete and deficient in unity.

90. What is the expanded relative form? Nothing but the sum of elementary expressions, or equations, of the first kind, such as 20 yards of linen=1 coat, 20 yards of linen=10 pounds of tea, etc.,

What does each of these equations imply? The corresponding inverted equations, 1 coat=20 yards of linen, 10 pounds of tea=20 yards of linen, etc.

91. In fact, when a person exchanges his linen for many other commodities, and thus expresses its value in a series of other commodities, it necessarily follows, that the various owners of the latter exchange them for linen, and consequently express the value of their various commodities in one and the same third commodity — linen.

If we give expression to the converse relation implied in the series, what do we get? The general form of value — Form C.

1 coat
10 pounds of tea g
40 pounds of coffee
1 quarter of corn
2 ounces of gold
1-2 ton of iron
X commodity A, etc.

=20 yards of linen

1. The altered character of the form of value.
92. How do all commodities now express their value?

First. — In an elementary form, because in a single commodity.

Second. — With unity, because in one and the same commodity.

Third. — This form of value is elementary and the same for all, therefore general.

93. The forms A and B were fit only to express the value of a commodity as something different from its use-value or material form.

94. When does the first form (A) practically occur? Only in the beginning, when products of labor are converted into commodities by accidental and occasional exchanges.

The first form A such as the following: 1 coat=20 yards of linen, 10 pounds of tea, 1-2 ton of iron, the value of the coat is equated to the linen, that of the tea to the iron. But to be equated to linen, and again to iron, is to be as different as is linen and iron.

95. What does the second form (B) distinguish, in a more adequate manner than the first? The value of a commodity from its use-value; for the value of the coat is there placed in contrast, under all possible

shapes, with the bodily form of the coat, it is equated to linen, to iron, to tea, in short, to everything else, only not to itself—the coat.

On the other hand, any general expression of value common to all is directly excluded; for, in the equation of value of each commodity, all other commodities appear only under the form of equivalents.

When does the expanded form of value, for the first time, come into existence? So soon as a particular product of labor, such as cattle, is no longer occasionally, but habitually, exchanged for other commodities.

96. How does the third, and last developed, form express the values of the world of commodities? In terms of a single commodity, set apart for that purpose—namely, the linen.

How do all other commodities represent their values? By means of their equality with linen.

The value of every commodity is now, by being equated to the linen, not only differentiated from its use-value, but from all other use-values generally, and is by that very fact expressed as that which is common to all other commodities.

How are commodities made to appear as values? By this—general—form commodities are, for the first time, effectually brought into relation with each other as values, or made to appear as values.

97. The two earlier forms either express the value of each commodity in terms of a single commodity of a different kind, or in a series of many such commodities.

In both cases it is, so to say, the special business of each single commodity to find an expression of its value; and this it does without the help of the others.

These others, without respect for the former, play the passive part of equivalents.

The general form C results from the joint action of the world of commodities and from that alone.

How can a commodity acquire a general expression of its value? Only by all other commodities, simultaneously with it, expressing their values in the same equivalent. And every new commodity must follow suit.

What does this make evident? That, since the existence of commodities as values is purely social, this social existence can be expressed by the totality of their social relation alone.

What, then, must the form of their value be? A socially recognized form.

98. How do all commodities, being now equated to linen, appear? Not only as qualitatively equal as values generally, but also as values whose magnitudes are capable of comparison. And by expressing the magnitude of their values in the same material—linen—those magnitudes are also compared to each other.

For instance, 10 pounds of tea=20 yards of linen, and 40 pounds of coffee=20 yards of linen, therefore, 10 pound of tea=40 pounds of coffee.

In other words, there is contained in one pound of coffee only one-fourth as much substance of value—labor—as is contained in one pound of tea.

99. What does the general form of relative value convert the single commodity, that acts as equivalents, into? The universal equivalent.

In our case, the linen is excluded from the rest and made to play the part of equivalent to all other commodities.

What does the bodily form of linen now assume to be? The form assumed in common by the value of all other commodities.

What does the substance—linen—become? The visible incarnation, the social crysalis state of every kind of human labor.

Weaving, which is the labor of certain private individuals producing a particular article, linen, acquires in consequence a social character—the character of equality with all other kind of human labor.

The innumerable equations of which the general form of value is composed, equate in turn the labor embodied in the linen to that embodied in every other commodity, and thus they convert weaving into the general form, or manifestation of undifferentiated human labor.

In this manner the labor realized in the value of commodities is represented, not only in its negative aspect, under which abstraction is made from every concrete form and useful property of actual work, but its own positive nature is made to reveal itself expressly.

What do we see by the general value form? That all kinds of actual labor is reduced to their common character of being human labor generally—of being the expenditure of human labor power.

100. What else does the general form show? That all labor possesses the character of being human labor, and of being specifically social in its character.

What constitutes its social character? Representing all products of labor as mere congealations of undifferentiated human labor, which shows by its very structure that it is the social resume of the world of commodities.

2. The interdependent development of the relative form of value and the equivalent form.

101. What does the degree of development of the relative value form correspond to? That of the equivalent.

But what must we bear in mind? That the development of the equivalent form is only the expression and result of the development of the relative value form.

102. The primary or isolated relative form of value of one commodity, converts some other commodity into an isolated equivalent.

The expanded form of relative value, which is the expression B of one commodity in terms of all other commodities, endows those commodities with the character of particular equivalents differing in kind.

And, lastly, why does a particular kind of commodity acquire the character of universal equivalent? Because all other commodities make it the material in which they uniformly express their value.

103. How is the antagonism between the relative form of value, and the equivalent form, developed? The two poles of the value form are developed concurrently with this form itself.

104. Why is it difficult to grasp the polar contrast from the first value form — 20 yards of linen: 1 coat? Because, as we read this equation backwards or forwards the parts played by the linen and the coat are different.

In the one case, the relative value of the linen is expressed in the coat; in the other case the relative value of the coat is expressed in the linen.

Their position in the equation being changeable makes it difficult to grasp the polar contrast.

105. What does form B show us? That only one single commodity can, at a time, completely expand its relative value. How does it acquire this expanded form? Only because, and in so far as, all other commodities are, with respect to it, equivalents.

What would result from reversing the equation in form B? It would convert it into the general form of value C.

106. What does the general form of value C give to the world of commodities? A general social relative form of value, because, and in so far as, thereby all commodities, except one, are excluded from the equivalent form. A single commodity, the linen, appears therefore to have acquired the character of direct exchangeability with every other commodity, because, and in so far as, this character is denied to every other commodity.

107. The commodity that figures as universal equivalent is, on the other hand, excluded from the relative value form.

If the linen, or any other commodity serving as universal equivalent, were at the same time to share in the relative form of value, it would have to serve as its own equivalent; we should then have 20 yards of linen=20 yards of linen. This tautology expresses neither value nor magnitude of value.

In order to express the relative value of the universal equivalent, we must rather reverse the form C.

This equivalent has no relative form of value in common with other commodities, but its value is relatively expressed by a never-ending series of other commodities.

Thus the expanded form of value, or form B, shows itself as the specific form of relative value for the equivalent commodity.

3. Transition from the general form of value to the money form.

108. What is the universal form of value? It is a form of value in general.

What commodity can assume this form? Any commodity.

On the other hand, if a commodity be found to have assumed the universal equivalent (form C) this is only because, and in so far as, it has been excluded from the rest of all other commodities as their equivalent, and that by their own act.

When does the general form of relative value obtain real consistency and social validity? From the moment that this exclusion becomes finally restricted to one particular commodity, and from that moment only, does the general form of relative value of the world of commodities obtain real consistency and social validity.

109. What becomes the money form of commodities? The particular commodity with whose bodily form the equivalent form is thus socially identified.

What is the social function of that commodity? To play, within the world of commodities, the part of universal equivalent.

What commodity has attained the position of universal equivalent? Gold.

Among the commodities which, in form B, figured as particular equivalent of the linen, and in form C, express in common their relative values in linen, the foremost place has been obtained by one in particular — namely, gold.

How do we get the money form? In form C we replace the linen by gold, and get form D.

D. *The money form.*
20 yards of linen
1 coat
10 pounds of tea
40 pounds of coffee
1 quarter of corn
1-2 ton of iron
X commodity A
=2 ounces of gold, or approximately $40.00. Hence the universal equivalent in this country is $.

110. In passing from form A to form B the changes are fundamental.

On the other hand, there is no difference between form C and D except that, in the latter gold has assumed the equivalent form in the place of the linen.

Gold in form D is, what linen was in form C, the universal equivalent.

The progress consists in this alone, that the character of direct and universal exchangeability — in other words, that the universal equivalent form — has now, by social custom, become finally identified with the substance gold.

111. Why is gold, with reference to all other commodities, money? Only because, it was previously, with reference to them, a simple commodity.

Like all other commodities, it was also capable of serving as an equivalent, either as simple equivalent in isolated exchanges, or as particular equivalent by the side of others.

How did gold become the money form? Gradually it began to serve, within varying limits, as universal equivalent.

So soon as it monopolizes this position in the expression of value of the world of commodities, it becomes the money commodity and then, and not till then, does form D become distinct from form C and the general form of value become changed into the money form.

112. What is the price form of a commodity? The elementary expression of the relative value of a single commodity, such as linen, in terms of a commodity, such as gold, that plays the part of money, is the price form of that commodity.

The price form of the linen is, therefore, 20 yards of linen: 2 ounces of gold, or if 2 ounces of gold, when coined are $40, then 20 yards of linen=$40.

113. What is the difficulty in forming a concept of the money form? That of clearly comprehending the universal equivalent form, and, as a necessary corollary, the general form of value, form C, the latter is deduced from form B, the expanded form of value, the essential component element of which, we saw, is form A, 20 yards of linen=1 coat, or X commodity A=Y commodity B.

What is the germ of the money form? This simple commodity form.

Section 4. The fetishism of commodities and the secret thereof.

114. A commodity appears, a first sight, a very trivial thing, and easily understood.

Its analysis shows that it is, in reality, a very queer thing, abounding in metaphysical subtleties, and theological niceties.

So far as it a value in use, there is nothing mysterious about it, whether we consider it from the point of view that by it properties it is capable of satisfying human wants, or from the point that those properties are the product of human labor.

It is as clear as noon-day that man, by his industry, changes the forms of the material furnished by nature in such a way as to make them useful to him.

The form of wood, for instance, is altered by making a table out of it, yet for all that, the table continues to be that common everyday thing—wood.

But, so soon as it steps forth as a commodity, it is changed into something transcendent.

It not only stands with its feet on the ground, but, in relation to other commodities, it stands on its head, and evolves out of its wooden brains grotesque ideas, far more wonderful than the table-turning ever was.

115. The mystical character of commodities does not originate, therefore, in their use-values.

Just as little does it proceed from the nature of the determining factors of value.

For, in the first place, however varied the useful kinds of labor, or productive activities may be, it is a physiological fact that they are functions of the human organism, and that each such function, whatever may be its nature or form, is essentially the expenditure of human brains, nerves, muscles, etc.

Secondly, with regard to that which forms the ground-work for the quantitative determination of value, namely, the duration of that expenditure, or the quantity of labor, it is quite clear that there is a palpable difference between its quantity and its quality.

In all states of society, the labor time that it costs to produce the means of subsistence must necessarily be of interest to mankind, though not of equal interest in different stages of development.

And, lastly, from the moment that men in any way work for one another, their labor assumes a social form.

How is the equality of all sorts of human labor expressed? Objectively—by their products all being equally values.

What takes the form of the quantity of value of the products of labor? The measure of the expenditure of labor power by duration of that expenditure.

Finally, what form does the mutual relation of the producers, within which the social character of their labor affirms itself, take? The form of a social relation between the products.

116. Why is a commodity a mysterious thing? Simply because the social character of men's labor appear to them as an objective character stamped upon the product of that labor; because the relation of the producers to the sum total of their own labor is presented to them as a social relation existing not between themselves, but between the products of their labor.

This is the reason why the products of labor become commodities, social things whose qualities are at the same time perceptible and imperceptible by the senses.

In the same way the light from an object is perceived by us not as the subjective excitation of the optic nerve, but as the objective form of something outside the eye itself.

NOTE—The rays of light reflected from an object on the eye stimulates the nerves and causes them to vibrate.

On the inner end of the nerves there are bulbs, in which the vibrations discharge.

This nervous discharge causes a movement of the medulla over a certain path on the brain, and produces what we call "the image. "

To perceive is to recognize the sense impressions, or nervous discharge; we, therefore, perceive, not the object, but the sense impressions caused by the reflection of light from the object to the eye.

But, in the act of seeing, there is, at all events, an actual passage of light from one thing to another, from the external object to the eye.

There is a physical relation between physical things.

How is it with commodities? Entirely different.

There the existence of things as commodities, and the value relation between the products of labor which stamps them as commodities, have absolutely no connection with their physical properties and with the material relation arising therefrom.

There it is a definite social relation between men that assumed, in their eyes, the fantastic form of a relation between things.

In order, therefore, to find an analogy, we must have recourse to the mist-enveloped regions of the religious world.

In that world the products of the human brain appear as independent beings endowed with life, and enter into relation both with one another and the human race.

So it is with the world of commodities, with the products of men's hands.

This I call the fetishism which attaches itself to the products of labor, so soon as they are produced as commodities, and which is, therefore, inseparable from the production of commodities.

117. This fetishism of commodities has its origin, as our foregoing analysis has already shown, in the peculiar social character of the labor that produces them.

118. Why do articles, as a general rule, become commodities? Only because they are products of the labor of private individuals who carry on their work independently of each other.

The sum total of the labor of these private individuals forms the aggregate labor of society.

Since the producers do not come into social contact with each other until they exchange their products, the specific social character of each producer's labor does not show itself except in the act of exchange.

In other words, the labor of the individual asserts itself as part of the labor of society only by means of the relation which the act of exchange establishes directly between the products, and indirectly, through them, between the producers.

To the latter, therefore, the relation connecting the labor of one individual with the rest appears, not as direct and social relations between individuals at work, but as what they really are, material relations between persons, and social relations between things.

It is only by being exchanged that the products of labor acquire, as values, one uniform social status, distinct from their varied form of existence as objects of utility.

This division of a product into a useful thing and a value becomes practical only when exchange has acquired such an extension that useful articles are produced for the purpose of being exchanged, and their character as value has to be taken into account beforehand during production.

From this moment the labor of the individual producer acquires socially a two-fold character.

On the one hand, it must, as a definite useful kind of labor, satisfy a definite social want, and thus hold its place as a part and parcel of the collective labor of all, as a branch of the social division of labor that has sprung up spontaneously.

On the other hand, it can satisfy the manifold wants of the individual producer himself only in so far as the mutual exchangeability of all kinds of useful private labor is an established social fact, and therefore the private useful labor of each producer ranks on an equal with all others.

The equalization of the most different kinds of labor can be the result only of an abstraction from their inequalities, or of reducing them to their common denominator, namely, expenditure of human labor power, or human labor in the abstract. The two-fold social character of the labor of the individual appears to him, when reflected in his brain, only under the forms which are impressed upon the labor in every-day practice by the exchange of products.

In this way the character that his own labor possesses of being socially useful takes the form of the conditions that the products must be not only useful, but useful to others, and the social character that his particular labor has, of being equal to all other kinds of labor, takes the form that all the physically different articles that are the products of labor have one common quality, namely, that of having value.

119. Is it because we see in the product of our labor, articles that are the receptacles of homogeneous human labor that we bring them into relation with each other as values? On the contrary; whenever, by an exchange, we equate as values our different products, by that very act we also equate, as human labor, the different kinds of labor expended upon them.

We are not aware of this, but nevertheless we do it.

Value, therefore, does not stalk about with a label describing it.

It is value, rather, that converts every product into a social heiroglyphic.

Later on we try to decipher the heiroglyphic, to get behind the secret of our social products; for to stamp an object of utility as a value is just as much a social product as language.

The recent scientific discovery that the products of labor, so far as they are values, are but material expressions of human labor spent in their production, marks, indeed, an epoch in the history of the development of the human race, but by no means dissipates the mists through which the social character of labor appears to us to be an objective character of the products themselves.

What does this social character of private labor, carried on independently, consist in? The equality of every kind of that labor, by virtue of its being human labor; which character, therefore, assumes in the product the form of value—this fact appears to the producers, notwithstanding the discovery above referred to, to be just as real and final as the fact that, after the discovery, by science, of the component gases of the air, the atmosphere remained the same.

120. What, first of all, practically concerns producers when making an exchange is the question, how much of some other product they get for their own?

In what proportion the products are exchangeable? When these proportions have—by custom—attained a certain stability, they appear to result from the nature of the products, so that, for instance, one ton of iron and two ounces of gold, appear as naturally to be of equal value as a pound of gold and a pound of iron—in spite of their different physical and chemical properties—appear to be of equal weight.

The character of having value, when once impressed upon products, obtains fixity only by reason of their acting and reacting upon each other as quantities of value.

These quantities vary continually, independent of the will, foresight, and action of the producers.

To them their own social action takes the form of the action of the objects, which rule the producers instead of being ruled by them.

It requires a fully developed production of commodities before, from accumulated experience alone, the scientific conviction springs up that all the different kinds of private labor which are carried on independently of each other, and yet as spontaneous developed branches of the social division of labor, are continually being reduced to the quantitative proportion in which society requires them.

And why? Because in the midst of all the accidental and ever fluctuating exchange relation between the products, the labor-time socially necessary for their production forcibly asserts itself like an over-riding law of nature.

The law of gravity thus asserts itself when a house falls about our ears.

The determination of the magnitude of value by labor—time is, therefore, a secret, hidden under the apparent fluctuations in the relative value of commodities.

Its discovery, while removing all appearance of accidentality from the determination of the magnitude of the value of products, yet in no way alters the mode in which that determination takes place.

121. What course does man's reflection of social life, and his scientific analysis of these forms, take? Directly the opposite of their historical development.

Where does he begin? With the result of the processes of development ready to hand before him.

What is necessary before man seeks to decipher the meaning of commodities? The character that stamps products as commodities, and whose establishment is a necessary preliminary to the circulation of commodities, have already acquired the stability of natural self-understood forms of social life before man seeks to decipher, not the historical character, for in his eyes they are immutable, but their meaning.

What led to the determination of the magnitude of values? The analysis of the prices of commodities alone.

What led to the establishment of their characters as values? It was the common expression of all commodities in money.

What actually conceals, instead of disclosing the social character of private labor, and the social relation between the producers? The ultimate money form of the world of commodities.

When I stated that coats or boots stand in a relation to linen, because it is the incarnation of abstract human labor, the absurdity of the statement is self-evident.

Nevertheless, when the producers of coats and boots compare those articles with linen, or what is the same thing, with gold and silver, as the universal equivalent, they express the relation between their private labor and the collective labor of society in the same absurd forms.

122. The categories of bourgeois economy consists of such like forms.

They are forms of thought expressing with social validity the conditions and relations of a definite historically determined mode of production—namely, the production of commodities.

The whole mystery of commodities, all the magic and necromancy that surrounds the products of labor as long as they take the form of commodities, vanishes, therefore, so soon as we come to other forms of production.

123. Since Robinson Crusoe's experience is a favorite theme with political economists, let us take a look at him on his island.

Moderate though he be, yet some few wants he has to satisfy, and must therefore do a little work of various sorts, such as making tools, and furniture, taming goats, fishing and hunting, of his prayers and the like we will take no account, since they are a pleasure to him, and he looks upon them as so much recreation.

In spite of the variety of his work, he knows that his labor, whatever its form, is but the activity of one and the same Robinson and consequently consists of nothing but different modes of human labor.

Necessity compels him to apportion his time accurately between his different kinds of work. Whether one kind occupies a greater space in his general activity than another depends upon the difficulties, greater or less as the case may be, to overcome in attaining the useful effect aimed at.

This our friend Robinson soon learns by experience, and having rescued a watch, ledger, pen and ink, from the wreck, commences like a true born Briton, to keep a set of books.

His stock-book consists of a list of the objects of utility that belong to him, of the operations necessary for their production, and, lastly, the labor time that definite quantities of these objects have, on an average, cost him.

All the relations between Robinson and the objects that form his wealth, of his own creation, are here so simple and clear as to be intelligible without exertion.

124. Let us now transport ourselves from Robinson's island, bathed in light, to the European Middle Ages, shrouded in darkness.

Here, instead of the independent man, we find everyone dependent—serfs and lords, vassals and suzerains, laymen and clergy.

Personal dependence here characterizes the social relations of production just as much as it does the other spheres of life organized on the basis of that production.

But for the very reason that personal dependence forms the ground-work of society, there is no necessity for labor and its products to assume a fantastic form different from their reality.

They take the shape, in the transactions of society of service in kind and payment in kind.

Here the particular and natural form of labor, and not as in a society based on the production of commodities, its general abstract form is the immediate social form of labor.

Compulsory labor is just as properly measured by time as commodity producing labor; but every serf knows that what he spends in the service of his lord is a definite quantity of his own personal labor-power.

The tithe to be rendered to the priest is more matter of fact than his blessing.

No matter, then, what we may think of the parts played by the different classes of people in this society, the social relations between individuals in the performance of their labor appear, at all events, as their own mutual personal relations, and are not disguised under the social relations between the products of labor.

125. For an example of labor in common or directly associated labor, we have no occasion to go back to that spontaneously developed form which we find on the threshold of the history of civilized races.

We have one close at hand in the patriarchal industry of a peasant family, that produce corn, cattle, yarn, linen, and clothing for home use.

These different articles are, as regards the family, so many products of its labor, but as between themselves they are not commodities.

The different kinds of labor, such as tillage, cattle tending, spinning, weaving, and making clothes, which result in the various products, are in themselves, and such as they are, direct social functions, because functions of the family; which, just as much as a society based on the production of commodities, possesses a spontaneously-developed system of division of labor.

The distribution of the work within the family, and the regulation of the labor-time of the several members, depends as well upon difference of age and sex as upon natural conditions varying with the seasons.

The labor power of each individual, by its very nature, operates in this case merely as a definite portion of the whole labor power of the family; and therefore the expenditure of individual labor power by its duration appears here, by its very nature, as a social character of their labor.

126. Let us now picture to ourselves, by way of a change, a community of free individuals, carrying on their work with the means of production in common, in which the labor power of all the different individuals is consciously applied as the combined labor power of the community.

All the characteristics of Robinson's labor is here repeated, but with this difference, that they are social instead of individual.

Everything produced by him was the result of his own personal labor, and, therefore, simply an article of use for himself.

The total product of our community is a social product.

One portion serves as fresh means of production and remains social.

But another portion is consumed by the members as means of subsistence.

A distribution of this portion among them is consequently necessary.

The mode of this distribution will vary with the productive organization of the community, and the historical development attained by the producers.

We will assume, but merely for a parallel with the production of commodities, that the share of each individual producer in the means of subsistence is determined by his labor time.

Labor time would, in this case, play a double part; its apportionment in accordance with a definite social plan maintains the proper proportion between the different kinds of work to be done and the various wants of the community.

On the other hand, it also serves as a measure of the portion of the common labor borne by each individual, and his share in the total part of the product destined for individual consumption.

The social relation of the individual producers, with regard both to their labor and to its products, are, in this case, perfectly simple and intelligible, and that with regard not only to production, but also to distribution.

127. The religious world is but a reflex of the real world.

And for a society based upon the production of commodities, in which the producers in general enter into social relations with one another by treating their products as commodities and values, whereby they reduce their individual private labor to the standard of homogenous human labor—for such a society Christianity with its cults of abstract man, more especially in its bourgeois developments, protestantism, deism, etc., is the most fitting form of religion.

In the ancient Asiatic, and other ancient modes of production, we find that the conversion of products into commodities, and therefore the conversion of men into producers of commodities, holds a subordinate place, which, however, increases in proportion as primitive communities approaches nearer and nearer to their dissolution.

Trading nations; properly so-called, exist in the ancient world only in its interstices, like the gods of Epicurus, in the *intermuda*, or like the Jews in the pores of Polish society.

These ancient social organisms of production are, as compared with bourgeois society, extremely simple and transparent.

But they are founded either on the immature development of man individually, who has not yet severed the umbilical cord that unites him with his fellow-men in a primitive tribal community, or upon direct relation of subjection.

They can arise and exist only when the development of the productive power of labor has not risen beyond a low stage, and, when, therefore, the social relation within the sphere of material life between man and man, and between man and nature, are correspondingly narrow.

This narrowness is reflected in the ancient worship of nature, and in the other elements of the popular religions.

The religious reflex of the real world can, in any case, only then finally vanish when the practical relations of everyday life offer none but perfectly intelligible and reasonable relations with regard to his fellow-men and to nature.

128. The life process of society, which is based on the process of material production, does not strip off its mystical veil until it is treated as production of freely associated men, and is consciously regulated by them in accordance with a settled plan.

This, however, demands for society a certain material ground-work or set of conditions of existence which in their turn are the spontaneous product of a long and painful process of development.

129. Political economy has, indeed, analyzed, however incompletely, value and its magnitude, and has discovered what lies behind these forms.

But it has never once asked the question why labor is represented by the value of its product and labor time by the magnitude of that value.

These formulae, which bear stamped upon them, in unmistakable letters, that they belong to a state of society in which the process of production has the mastery over man, instead of being controlled by him. Such formulae appear, to the bourgeois intellect, to be as much a self-evident necessity imposed by nature as productive labor itself.

Hence forms of production that preceded the bourgeois form are treated by the bourgeois in much the same way as the Fathers of the Church treated pre-Christian religions.

130. To what extent some economists are misled by the objective appearance of the social characteristics of labor, is shown, among other ways, by the dull and tedious quarrel over the part played by nature in the formation of exchange-value.

Since exchange-value is a definite social manner of expressing the amount of labor bestowed upon an object, nature has no more to do with it than it has in fixing the course of exchange.

131. The mode of production in which the product takes the form of commodities, or is produced directly for exchange, is the most general and most embryonic form of bourgeois production.

It therefore makes its appearance at an early date in history, though not in the same predominating and characteristic manner as now-a-days.

Hence its fetish character is comparatively easy to be seen through.

But when we come to more concrete forms, even this appearance of simplicity vanishes.

Whence arose the illusions of the monetary system? To it, gold and silver, when serving as money, did not represent a social relation between producers, but mere natural objects, with strange social properties.

And modern economy, which looks down with such disdain on the monetary system, does not its superstition come out as clear as noon-day whenever it treats of capital? How long is it since economy discarded the physiocratic illusion that rents grew out of the soil, and not out of society.

132. But not to anticipate we will content ourselves with yet another example relating to the commodity form.

Could commodities themselves speak, they would say: Our use-value may be a thing that interests men. It is no part of us as objects. What, however, does belong to us as objects is our value. Our natural intercourse as commodities proves it.

Now listen how those commodities speak through the mouth of the economists:

"Value (i. e., exchange-value) is a property of things, riches (i, e., use-value) of man.

"Value, in this sense, necessarily implies exchanges; riches do not."

Riches (use-value) are the attribute of men; value is the attribute of commodities.

A man or a community is rich; a pearl or a diamond is valuable.

A pearl or a diamond is valuable as a pearl or a diamond.

So far, no chemist has ever discovered exchange-value in a pearl or a diamond.

The economic discoverers of this chemical element, who, by the by, lay special claim to critical acumen, find, however, that the use-value belongs to them independently of their material proper ties, while their value, on the other hand, form a part of them as objects.

What confirms them in this view is the peculiar circumstance that the use-value of objects is realized without exchange by means of a direct relation between the objects and man, while, on the other hand, their value is realized only by exchange; that is, by means of a social process.

Who fails here to call to mind our good friend Dogberry, who informs neighbor Seacoal that "to be a well favored man is the gift of fortune; but reading and writing comes by nature."

Chapter II. Exchange

133. It is plain that commodities cannot go to market and make exchange on their own account. We must, therefore, have recourse to their guardians, who are also their owners.

Commodities are things, and therefore without power of resistance against man. If they are wanting in docility he can use force; in other words, he can take possession of them.

How, then, may these objects enter into relation with each other as commodities? Their guardians must place themselves into relation as persons whose will resides in those objects, and must behave in such a way that each does not appropriate the commodity of the other and part with his own, except by means of an act done by mutual consent.

And what must they mutually recognize in each other? The rights of private proprietors.

What is this juridical relation which thus expresses itself in a contract, whether such contract be part of a legal system or not? It is a relation between two wills, and is but the reflex of the real economic relation between the two.

What does this economic relation determine? The subject matter comprised in such juridicial act.

How do the persons exist for one another? Merely as representatives of, and therefore as owners of, commodities.

In the course of our investigation we shall find, in general, that the characters who appear upon the economic stage are but the personifications of the economical relations that exists between them.

134. What chiefly distinguishes a commodity from its owner is the fact that it looks upon every other commodity as but the form of appearance of its own value.

A born leveler and a cynic, it is always ready to exchange not only soul, but body, with any and every other commodity, be the same more repulsive than Maritornes herself.

The owner makes up for this lack in a commodity of a sense of the concrete by his own five or more senses.

His commodity possesses for himself no immediate use-value. Otherwise he would not bring it to the market.

It has use-value for others; but for himself its only direct use-value is that of being a depository of exchange-value, and consequently a means of exchange.

Therefore, he makes up his mind to part with it for commodities whose value in use are of service to him.

All commodities are non-use-values for their owners, and use-values for their non-owners.

Consequently, they must all change hands.

But this change of hands is what constitutes their exchange, and the latter puts them in relation with each other as values, and realizes them as values.

Hence commodities must be realized as values, before they can be realized as use-values.

135. On the other hand, they must show that they are use-values before they can be realized as values.

How is it proved, whether the labor is useful for others, that the product will satisfy some want or other, or not? Only by the act of exchange.

136. Every owner of a commodity wishes to part with it in exchange for those commodities whose use-value satisfies some want of his.

Looked at in this way, what is exchange for him? Simply a private transaction.

On the other hand, he desires to realize the value of his commodity; to convert it into some suitable commodity of equal value, irrespective of whether his own commodity has or has not any use-value for the owner of the other.

From this point of view, what is exchange for him? A social transaction, of a general character.

But one and the same set of transactions can not be simultaneously, for all owners of commodities, both exclusively private and exclusively social and general.

137. To the owner of a commodity, what is every other commodity, in regard to his own? A particular equivalent.

What is his own commodity in regard to others? The universal equivalent.

But, since this applies to every owner, there is, in fact, no commodity acting as universal equivalent, and the relative value of commodities possesses no general form under which they can be equated as values, and have the magnitude of their values compared.

So far, therefore, they do not confront each other as commodities, but only as products or use-values.

In their difficulty our commodity owners think, like Faust, "In the beginning was the act."

They, therefore, acted and transacted before they thought. Instinctively they conform to the laws imposed by the nature of commodities.

How are commodities brought into relation as values, and therefore as commodities? Only by comparing them with some other commodity as the universal equivalent. That we saw from our analysis of a commodity.

But how can a particular commodity become the universal equivalent. Only by a social act.

How is this act performed? The social action of all other commodities set apart the particular commodity in which they all represent their values.

And, what becomes the form of the socially recognized universal equivalent? The bodily form of the commodity that is set apart to act as the universal equivalent.

What is the function of this commodity thus excluded from the rest? To act as their universal equivalent and it thus becomes money.

138. What is money? A crystal formed of necessity in the course of exchange, whereby different products of labor are practically equated to one another, and thus by practice are converted into commodities.

What does the historical progress and extension of exchanges develop? The contrast latent in commodities between use-value and value.

For what purpose is it necessary to give external expression to this contrast? Commercial intercourse.

What does this urge on? The establishment of an independent form of value, and finds no rest until it is once for all satisfied by the differentiation of commodities into commodities and money.

At the same rate, then, as the conversion of products into commodities is being accomplished, so also is the conversion of one special commodity into money.

NOTE—From this we may form an estimate of the shrewdness of the petite bourgeois socialism, which, while perpetuating the production of commodities, aims at abolishing the "antagonism" between money and commodities, and consequently, at abolishing money itself. We might just as well try to retain catholicism without the pope.

139. The direct barter of products attains the elementary form of the relative expression of value in one respect, but not in another. That form is X commodity A:Y commodity B.

How is this form, in direct barter, expressed? X use-value A=Y use-value B.

NOTE.—So long as, instead of two distinct use-values being exchanged, a chaotic mass of articles are offered as the equivalent of a single article, which is often the case with savages, even direct barter is in its infancy.

The articles A and B, in this case, are not as yet commodities; they become so only by the act of barter.

When is the first step made by an object of utility towards acquiring exchange value? When it forms a non-use-value for its owner.

When does this happen? When it forms a superfluous portion of some article required for his immediate use.

Objects in themselves are external to man, and, consequently, alienable by him.

What is necessary in order that this alienation may be reciprocal? For men, by a tacit understanding, to treat each other as private owners of these alienable objects, and by implication as independent individuals.

But such a state of reciprocal independence has no existence in a primitive society based on property in common, whether such a society takes the form of a patriarchal family, an ancient Indian community, or a Peruvian Inca state.

Where does the product of labor first begin to become commodities? On the boundaries of such communities, at the point of contact with other similar communities, or with members of the latter.

What happens to products when they have become commodities in the external relations of a community? They also, by reaction, become commodities in their internal intercourse.

What determines their exchange proportions at first? It is a mere matter of chance.

What makes them exchangeable? The desire of their owner to alienate them.

What makes exchange a normal social act? Constant repetition of exchange.

When is the distinction, between the utility of a thing for consumption and its utility for the purpose of exchange, established? In the course of time some portion, at least, of the product of labor must be produced with a special view to exchange.

From that moment use-value becomes distinguished from its exchange value.

On the other hand, upon what does the proportions in which the articles are exchanged depend? Production itself.

What stamps them as values with definite magnitudes? Custom.

140. What is each commodity, in direct barter, to its owner? A direct means of exchange.

What is it to all other persons? An equivalent, but only in so far as it has use-value for them.

At this stage, therefore, the articles exchanged do not acquire a value form independent of their own use-values, or of the individual needs of the exchangers.

The necessity of the value form grows with the increasing number and variety of the commodities exchanged.

The problem and means of solution rise simultaneously.

What is necessary for the exchange of commodities on a large scale? That all the different kinds of commodities be exchangeable for and equated to one and the same special article.

Commodity owners never equate their own commodities to those of others, and exchange them on a large scale, without different kinds of commodities belonging to different owners being exchangeable for, and equated as values to, one and the same special article.

What does this last mentioned article become? The equivalent of various other commodities, and thus acquires at once, though within narrow limits, the character of a general social equivalent.

Is this character permanent to one article? No; it comes and goes with the momentary social act that called it into life.

In turns and transiently it attaches itself first to this and then to that commodity.

How does it act, with the development of exchange? It fixes itself firmly and exclusively to particular sorts of commodities, and becomes crystalized by becoming the money form.

What determines the particular commodity to which it sticks at first? Mere accident.

What are the circumstances, whose influence decides, what article will take on the money-form? The money-form attaches itself either to the most important article of exchange from outside —and these, in fact, are primitive and natural forms in which the exchange-value of home products find expression—or else it attaches itself to the object of utility that form, like cattle, the chief portion of indigenous alienable wealth.

Who are the first to develop the money-form? The nomadic races.

Why? Because all their worldly goods consist of moveable objects, and are, therefore, directly alienable; and because their mode of life, by continually bringing them in contact with foreign communities, solicits the exchange of products.

Man has often made man himself, under the form of slaves, serve as primitive material for money, but has never used land for that purpose.

Where could such an idea spring up? Only in a bourgeois society already well developed.

It dates from the last third of the seventeenth century, and the first attempt to put it in practice on a national scale was made a century afterward, during the French bourgeois revolution.

141. How does the commodity best fitted, by nature, to perform the social function of a universal equivalent, attain that end? In proportion as exchange bursts its local bonds, and the values of commodities more and more expand into an embodiment of human labor in the abstract, in the same proportion the character of money attaches itself to commodities best fitted to perform the social function of a universal equivalent.

What commodities are these? The precious metals.

142. The truth of the proposition that "although gold and silver are not by nature money, money is by nature gold and silver" is shown by the fitness of the physical properties of these metals for the function of money.

Up to this point, however, we are acquainted with only one function of money; namely, to serve as the form of manifestation of the values of commodities, or as the material in which the magnitude of their values are socially expressed.

What material will give an adequate form of the manifestation of value — a fit embodiment of abstract, undifferentiated, and, therefore, equal human labor? That material alone, whose every sample exhibits the same uniform quality.

What other quality must it also possess? Since the difference between the magnitudes of value is purely quantitative, it must be divisible at will, and equally capable of being united.

What materials possess these qualities? Gold and silver.

143. What does the use-value of money become? Two-fold. In addition to its special use-value as a commodity (gold, for instance, serving to fill teeth, to form the raw materials of articles of luxury, etc.), it acquires a formal use-value, originating in its special social function.

How do commodities act as regards the universal equivalent? They play the part of particular commodities.

Since all commodities are mere equivalents of money, the latter being their universal equivalent, they with regard to the latter as the universal commodity, play the parts of particular commodities.

144. We have seen that the money form is but the reflex, thrown upon one single commodity, of the value relations between all the rest.

That money is a commodity is, therefore, a new discovery only for those who, when they analyze it, start from its fully-developed shape.

The act of exchange gives to the commodity converted into money, not its value, but its specific value—form.

What has the confounding of these two distinct things, led some writers to hold? That the value of gold and silver is imaginary.

NOTE—Locke says: "The universal consent of mankind gives to silver on account of its qualities which made it suitable for money, an imaginary value."

Law, on the other hand, "How could different nations give an imaginary value to any single thing . . . or how could their imaginary value maintain itself?"

But the following shows how little he himself knew about the matter: "Silver was exchanged in proportion to the value in use it possessed, consequently, in proportion to its real value. By its adoption as money, it received an additional value." (Jean Law in E Daires edit. of *Economic Financiers du XVIII Siecle*)

What gave rise to that other mistaken notion that money itself is a mere symbol of value? The fact that in certain functions it can be replaced by mere symbols.

Nevertheless, under this error lurked the presentiment that the money-form of an object is not an inseparable part of that object, but is simply the form under which certain social relations manifest themselves.

In what sense is every commodity a symbol of value? In so far as it is value, it is only the material envelop of the human labor spent upon it.

But, if it be declared that the social characters assumed by objects, or the material forms assumed by the social qualities of labor under the regime of a definite mode of production, are mere symbols, it is in the same breath also declared that these characteristics are arbitrary fictions sanctioned by the so-called universal consent of mankind.

This suited the mode of explanation in favor during the eighteenth century.

Unable to account for the origin of the puzzling forms assumed by social relations between man and man, people sought to denude them of their strange appearance by ascribing to them a conventional origin.

145. It has already been remarked above that the equivalent form of a commodity does not imply the determination of the magnitude of its value.

Therefore, although we may be aware that gold is money, and consequently directly exchangeable for all other commodities, yet that fact by no means tell us how much 10 pounds, for instance, of gold, is worth.

Money, like every other commodity, cannot express the magnitude of its value except relatively in other commodities.

Then how is the value of money determined? By the labor time required for its production.

And how is it expressed? By the quantity of any other commodity that costs the same amount of labor time.

Where does such quantitative determination take place? At the source of its production — the mines.

How does it take place? By means of barter. When it steps into circulation as money its value is already given.

In the last decades of the seventeenth century, it had already been shown that money is a commodity, but this step marks only the infancy of the analysis.

The difficulty lies, not in comprehending that money is a commodity, but in discovering how, why, and by what means a commodity becomes money.

146. Summary — We have already seen, from the most elementary expression of value, X commodity A=Y commodity B, that the object in which the magnitude of the value of another object is represented appears to have the equivalent form independent of this relation as a social property given to it by nature.

We follow up this false appearance to its final establishment, which is complete so soon as the universal equivalent form becomes identified with the bodily form of a particular commodity, and thus crystalized into the money-form.

What appears to happen is not that gold becomes money in consequence of all other commodities expressing their values in it, but on the contrary, that all other commodities express their value in gold because it is money.

The intermediate steps vanish in the results and leave no trace behind.

Commodities find their own value already represented without any initiation on their part, in another commodity existing in company with them.

These objects, gold and silver, just as they come out of the bowels of the earth, are forthwith the direct incarnation of all human labor.

Hence the magic of money.

In the form of society now under consideration the behavior of men in the social process of production is purely atomic.

Hence their relation to each other in production assumes a material character independent of their control and conscious individual action.

These facts manifest themselves at first by products taking the form of commodities.

We have seen how the progressive development of a society of commodity producers stamps one privileged commodity with the character of money.

Hence the riddle presented by money is but the riddle presented by commodities, only it now strikes us in it most glaring form.

Chapter III. Money, Or The Circulation Of Commodities

Section 1. The measure of values.

147. Throughout this work I assume, for the sake of simplicity, gold as the money commodity.

What is the first chief function of money? To supply commodities with the material for the expression of their values, or to represent their values as magnitudes of the same denomination, qualitatively equal, and quantitatively comparable.

It thus serves as a universal measure of value.

And only by virtue of this function does gold, the equivalent commodity *par excellance*, become money.

148. Is it money that renders commodities commensurable? Just on the contrary. It is because all commodities, as values, are realized human labor, and therefore commensurable, that their values can be measured by one and the same special commodity, and the latter be converted into the common measure of their value; that is, into money.

What is money as the measure of value? It is the phenomenal form that must of necessity be assumed by that measure of value which is imminent in commodities—labor-time.

NOTE—The question, why does not money directly represent labor-time, so that a piece of paper may represent, for instance, X hours labor? Is at bottom the same as the question why, given the production of commodities, must products take the form of commodities? This is evident, since their taking the form of commodities implies their differentiation into commodities and money, or why cannot private labor—labor for the account of private individuals—be treated as its opposite, immediate social labor? I have elsewhere examined thoroughly the Utopian idea of "paper money," in a society founded on the production of commodities.

On this point I will only say, further, that Owens' "labor money," for instance, is no more "money" than a ticket for the theater. Owen presupposes directly associated labor, a form of production that is entirely inconsistent with production of commodities.

The certificate of labor is merely evidence of the part taken by the individual in the common labor, and of his rights to a certain portion of the common produce destined for consumption. But, it never inters into Owens' head to presuppose the production of commodities, and at the same time, by juggling with money, to try to evade the necessary conditions of that production.

149. What is the money-form or price of a commodity? The expression of the value of a commodity in gold—X commodity A=Y money commodity.

What is now sufficient to express the value of a commodity in a socially valid manner? A single equation, such as 1-2 ton of iron: 2 ounces of gold.

Why is there no longer any need for this equation to figure as a link in the equations that express the values of all other commodities? Because the equivalent now has the character of money.

What has the general form of relative value resumed? Its original shape of isolated relative value.

What, on the other hand, has the endless series of equations, the expanded expressions of relative value, become? The form peculiar to the relative value of the money commodity.

The series itself, too, is now given, and has social recognition in prices of actual commodities.

How do we find the magnitude of the value of money expressed? In all sorts of commodities, by reading the quotation of the price list backwards.

What is the price of money? It has no price.

What would we have to do, in order to put it on an equal footing with all other commodities in this respect? Equate it to itself, which is no expression of value.

150. What is the price, or money-form of commodities? Like the form of value generally, a form quite distinct from their palpable bodily form; it is therefore a purely ideal or mental form.

How is value that has actual existence in commodities made ideally perceptible? By their equation with gold.

Although invisible, the value of iron, linen and corn has actual existence in these very articles; it is ideally made perceptible by their equality with gold — a relation that, so to say, exists only in their own heads.

How are the prices of commodities communicated to the outside world? Their owner must lend them his tongue or hang a ticket on them.

Since the expression of the value of commodities in gold is merely an ideal act, what may we use for that purpose? Imaginary or ideal money.

When and how do we employ money as imaginary or ideal money? When estimating and measuring the value of goods.

Every trader knows that he is far from having turned his goods into money when he has expressed their value in a price, or imaginary money, and that it does not require the least bit of gold to estimate, in that metal, millions of dollars worth of goods. This circumstance has given rise to the wildest theories.

But, although the money that performs the function of a measure of values is only ideal money, upon what does price depend? Entirely upon the actual substance that is money. How can we measure the value of commodities by an imaginary thing? The value — the quantity of human labor — contained in a ton of iron is expressed in imagination by such a quantity of the money commodity as contains the same amount of labor as the iron.

Would it cut any figure in the price, whether we use gold, silver or copper as the measure of value of the iron? The value of the iron would be expressed by very different prices, or will be represented by very different quantities of these metals respectively.

151. What would the result be, if we have two different measures of value, such as gold and silver, at the same time? All commodities would have two prices, a gold price and a silver price.

NOTE—This did really occur in the eighteen-seventies; you could purchase, from the grocer, one dollar's worth of goods, give a twenty dollar gold piece, and he would give you back twenty dollars in silver.

The prices of goods were $19 in gold and $20 in silver.

All notes were made payable in gold; $100 in gold were worth $105 in silver.

These exist quietly side by side so long as the ratio of the value of silver to that of gold remain unchanged—say 16 to 1.

Every change in the ratio disturbs the ratio which exists between the gold prices and the silver prices of commodities, and thus proves the fact that a double standard of value is inconsistent with the function of a standard.

152. How does the value of all commodities become magnitudes of the same denomination? Commodities with definite prices reesent themselves under the form: a commodity A=X gold; a commodity B=Z gold; c commodity C-=Y gold, etc.; where a. b. c. represent definite quantities of commodities A B C; X Z Y represent definite quantities of gold.

The value of these commodities are, therefore, changed in imagination into so many different quantities of gold.

Hence in spite of the confusing variety of the commodities themselves, their values become magnitudes of the same denomination—gold magnitudes.

They are now capable of being compared with each other and measured, and the want becomes technically felt of comparing them with some fixed quantity of gold as a unit of measure.

This unit, by subsequent divisions into aliquot parts, becomes itself the standard or scale.

Before they become money, gold, silver and copper already possess such standard of measures in their standards of weight; so that, for example, a pound weight, while serving as the unit, is, on the one hand, divisible into ounces, and on the other hand, may be combined to make up hundred weights.

It is owing to this that in all the metalic currencies the names given to the standards of money were originally taken from their pre-existing standards of weight.

Two functions of money.

153. As a measure of value and a standard of price, money has two entirely different functions to perform.

What is money as a measure of value? The socially recognized incarnation of human labor.

What is money as a standard of price? A fixed weight of metal.

How does money act as a measure of value? It converts the values of all the manifold commodities into prices, into imaginary quantities of gold.

How does money act as a standard of price? It measures those quantities of gold.

How does the measure of value measure commodities? Considered as values.

How does the standard of price measure the quantities of gold? By a unit quantity of gold.

Not the value of one quantity of gold by the weight of another.

What is necessary to make gold a standard of price? To fix upon a certain weight as a unit.

In this, as in all other cases, of measuring quantities of the same denomination, the establishment of an unvarying unit is all important.

Hence, the less the unit is subject to variation, so much the better does the standard of price fulfill its office.

But only in so far as it is itself the product of labor, and, therefore, potentially variable in value, can gold serve as a measure of value.

154. Does a change in the value of gold, in any way affect its function as a standard of price? None whatever; for no matter how this value varies the proportions between the values of different quantities remain constant.

However great the fall in its value, 12 ounces of gold still contain 12 times the value of one ounce, and in prices the only thing considered is the relation between different quantities of gold.

Since no rise or fail in the value of gold can alter its weight, no alteration can take place in its aliquot parts.

Thus gold always renders the same service as an invariable standard of price, however much its value may vary.

155. In the second place, a change in the value of gold does not interfere with its function as a measure of value.

The change affects all commodities simultaneously, and, therefore, other things being equal, leaves their relative value between themselves unaltered, although those values are now expressed in higher or lower gold prices.

156. Just as when we estimate the value of any commodity by a definite quantity of the use-value of some other commodity, so in estimating the former in gold, we assume nothing more than that the production of a given quantity of gold costs, at the given period, a given amount of human labor.

As regards the fluctuations of prices generally, they are subjected to the laws of relative value investigated in a former chapter.

157. How may a general rise in the prices of commodities occur? Only, either from a rise in their value, the value of money remaining constant, or from a fall in the value of money, the value of commodities remaining constant.

How may a general fall in the prices of commodities occur? Only from a fall in the value of commodities, the value of gold remaining constant, or from a rise in the value of money, the value of commodities remaining constant.

It therefore by no means follows that a rise in the value of money necessarily implies a proportional fall in the prices of commodities; or that a fall in the value of money implies a proportional rise in prices.

If their value rise slower or faster than that of money, the fall or rise in their, prices will be determined by the difference between the change in their value and that of the money, and so on.

Let us go back to the consideration of the price-form.

158. By degrees there arises a discrepancy between the current money names and the various weights of the precious metal figuring as money, and the actual weight which those names originally represented.

This discrepancy is the result of historical causes, among the chief are:

First.—The importation of foreign money into an imperfectly developed community.

This happened in Rome in its early days, where gold and silver coin circulated at first as foreign commodities.

The names of those foreign coins never coincided with that of the indigenous weights.

Second. —As wealth increases, the less precious metals are thrust out by the more precious from their place as a measure of value— copper by silver, silver by gold—however much this order of sequence may be in contradiction with poetical chronology.

The word *pound*, for instance, was the money name given to an actual pound weight of silver.

When gold replaced silver as a measure of value, the same name was applied according to the ratio between the values of silver and gold, to, perhaps, one-fifteenth part of a pound of gold.

The word pound, as a money name, thus became differentiated from the same word as a weight name.

NOTE—It is thus that the pound sterling in English denotes less than one-third of its original weight; the pound Scot, before the union, only one thirty-sixth; the French *livre* one-seventy-fourth; the Spanish *maravedi* less than one-thousandth; and the Portuguese *rei* a still smaller fraction.

Third.—The debasing of money carried on for centuries by kings and princes to such an extent that nothing, in fact, remained but the names.

159. These historical causes convert the separation of the money-name from the weight name into an established habit with the community.

Since the standard of money is, on the one hand, purely conventional, and must, on the other hand, find general acceptance, it is in the end regulated by law.

A given weight of one of the precious metals, an ounce of gold, for instance, becomes officially divided into aliquot parts, with legally bestowed names, such as pounds, dollars, and so forth.

These aliquot parts, which henceforth serve as units of money, are then subdivided into other aliquot parts, with legal names such as shilling, penny, etc.

Both before and after these divisions are made a definite weight of metal is the standard of metallic money.

The sole alteration consists in the subdivision and denomination.

160. The price, or quantity of gold, into which the value of commodities are ideally changed, are, therefore, expressed in the names of coins; or in the legally valid names of the subdivisions of the gold standard.

Hence, instead of saying: a quarter of wheat is worth an ounce of gold, we say it is worth £3, 17s, 10 1/2d.

In this way commodities express by their prices how much they are worth, and money serves as money of account whenever it is a question of fixing the value of an article in its money-form.

161. The name of a thing is something different from the qualities of that thing.

I know nothing of a man by knowing that his name is Jacob.

In the same way with regard to money—every trace of a value relation disappears in the name dollar, pound, franc, ducat, etc.

The confusion caused by attributing a hidden meaning to these cabalistic signs is all the greater because their money-names express both the values of commodities and, at the same time, aliquot parts of the weight of the metal that is in the standard of money.

On the other hand, it is absolutely necessary that value, in order that it may be distinguished from the various bodily forms of commodities, should assume this material and unmeaning, but, at the same time, purely social form.

162. What is price? The money-name of the labor realized in a commodity.

Hence, the expression of the equivalence of a commodity with the sum of money constituting its price, is tautology just as in general the expression of the relative value of a commodity is a statement of the equivalence of two commodities.

What is price the exponent of? The exchange ratio of a commodity with money.

Although price, being the exponent of the magnitude of a commodity's value, is the exponent of its exchange ratio with money, it does not follow that the exponent of this exchange ratio is necessarily the exponent of the commodities value.

Suppose two equal quantities of socially necessary labor to be respectfully represented by one quarter of wheat and £2.

£2 is the expression in money of the magnitude of the value of the quarter of wheat, or is its price.

If new circumstances allow of this price being raised to £3, or compel it to be reduced to £1, then, although £1 and £3 may be too small or too great to properly express the magnitude of the wheat's value, nevertheless they are its price.

For they are, in the first place, the form under which its value appears, that is money; and, in the second place, the exponent of its exchange ratio with money.

If the condition of production, in other words, if the productive power of labor remain constant, the same amount of social labor time must, both before and after the change in price, be expended in the production of a quarter of wheat.

This circumstance depends neither on the will of the wheat producers nor that of the owners of other commodities.

163. What does magnitude of value express? A relation of social production.

It expresses the relation that necessarily exists between a certain article and the portion of the total labor-time of society required to produce it.

As soon as magnitude of value is converted into price, the above necessary relation takes the shape of a more or less accidental exchange ratio between a single commodity and another, the money commodity.

But this exchange ratio may express either the magnitude of the commodity's value, or the quantity of gold deviating from that value, for which, according to circumstances it may be parted with.

The possibility, therefore, of quantitative incongruity between price and magnitude of value, or the deviation of the former from the latter, is inherent in the price-form itself.

This is no defect, but on the contrary, admirably adapts the price form to a mode of production whose inherent laws impose themselves only as the means of apparently lawless irregularities that compensate one another.

164. The price-form, however, is not only compatible with the possibility of a quantitative incongruity between magnitude of value and price, that is between the former and money, but it may also conceal quantitative inconsistency—so much so that although money

is nothing but the value-form of commodities, prices cease altogether to express value.

Objects that in themselves are no commodities, such as conscience, honor, etc., are capable of being offered for sale by their holders, and acquiring, through their price, the form of commodities.

Hence an object may have a price without having value.

The price in this case is imaginary, like certain quantities in mathematics.

On the other hand, the imaginary price-form may sometimes conceal either a direct or an indirect real value-relation; for instance the price of uncultivated land, which is without value, because no human labor has been incorporated in it.

165. What does price express? Price, like relative value in general, expresses the value of a commodity; for example, a ton of iron, by stating that a given quantity of the equivalent, for example an ounce of gold, is directly exchangeable for iron.

What must a commodity do in order to act effectually as exchange value in practice? Quit its bodily shape, transform itself from mere imaginary into real gold, although to the commodity such transubstantiation may be more difficult than the Hegelian "concept", the transition from "necessity" to "freedom", or to a lobster the casting of his shell, or to St. Jerome the putting off of old Adam.

NOTE—Jerome had to wrestle hard, not only in his youth with the bodily flesh, as shown by his fight in the desert with the handsome woman of his imagination, but also in his old age with the spiritual flesh. "I thought," he says, "I was in the spirit before the Judge of the universe." "Who art thou," asked a voice. "I am a Christian." "Thou liest," thundered back the Judge; "Thou art naught but a Ciceronian."

Though a commodity may, side by side with its actual form (iron, for instance,) take in our imagination the form of gold, yet it cannot at the same time actually be both iron and gold.

To fix its price it is sufficient to equate it to gold in imagination.

But to render its owner the service of a universal equivalent, it must be actually replaced by gold.

If the owner of the iron were to go to the owner of some other commodity offered for exchange, and were to refer him to the price of the iron as proof that it was already money, he would get the same answer as St. Peter gave, in heaven to Dante, when the latter recited the creed—"*Assai bene e trascorsa.*"

That's all very well, you have the proper alloy and the legal weight, but have you got it in your pocket?

166. A price, therefore, implies both that a commodity is exchangeable for money, and also that it must be so exchanged.

On the other hand, gold serves as an ideal measure of value only because it has already, in the process of exchange, established itself as the money commodity.

Under the ideal measure of value, there lurks the hard cash.

What has our analysis shown a commodity to be? An object outside us, that, by its properties satisfies some human want, that is the product of human labor, and placed in exchange relation with other commodities.

What are the elements of a commodity? Matter and labor.

What is most essential to a commodity? Being placed in the exchange relation.

Why so? Because a thing may be the product of human labor, a useful article, and if produced only for use, and not put in exchange relation it is not a commodity.

Being placed in, or being produced with a view of, exchange alone makes it a commodity.

On the other hand, a thing that has none of the properties of a commodity—is not the product of labor—take the form of a commodity on being exchanged for a commodity, that is money.

What has our analysis shown value to be? Simply a mode of expression. It expresses homogeneous labor in the abstract.

Magnitude of value expresses a definite quantity of value.

The magnitude of value is determined by the amount of labor-time socially necessary to produce the necessary quantity of an article to satisfy the wants of society.

What has our analysis shown price to be? The money-name for the labor embodied in a commodity.

It is the exponent of the exchange ratio between a single commodity and money.

It may or may not, according to circumstances represent the real value of an article.

It is the ideal value form.

What has our analysis shown regarding the law that regulates prices? The law that governs prices, or the exchange proportions of commodities, is value.

NOTE—To illustrate this seeming contradiction, let us take a physical law, for Marx says:

"The law of value is in economics what the law of gravity is in physics."

While all commodities are subject to the law of value, just as all bodies are subject to the law of gravitation, there are in both cases perturbations, which, when examined, afford further proof of the truth and universality of the law.

For example according to the law of gravity, all bodies raised in the air, fall to the earth in a direct line with its center.

Yet if the wind blows, the line of descent of the falling body, will be more or less oblique, according to the strength of the wind. A projectile describes a parabola which is the "resultant" of the force of projection and the force of gravity, variously modified by the resistance of the air, the form and density of the missile, and other factors. A balloon filled with a gas lighter than air rises in the air instead of falling, but in a vacuum it falls.

Again, in the air a piece of iron falls much more swiftly than a feather, but in a vacuum all bodies fall at the same rate of speed, etc. Not only are all these apparent "contradictions" readily explained, but the great perturbations in the heavens, examined in the light of the law of gravity, have enabled astronomers to discover the location and motion of planets and stars, whose existence was previously unsuspected.

Again, a plumb bob, we say, points to the center of gravity. Now everyone knows that a plumb bob is seldom at rest, it mostly swings to and fro.

A force, say the hand of a person, or the wind, moves the plumb bob in the direction in which the force is applied, but gravity asserts itself and pulls it back, so soon as the force is removed, not only to the center, but past it, and so it will swing to and fro until the force stored up in it is exhausted, and the bob will point to the center of gravity.

Now if we take the distance and number of swings made by the bob, on each side of the center line, we will find one equals the other, and that during the struggle between the force and resistance (gravity), gravity had at least maintained an average of center in spite of the disturbance. And it is this deviation that proves gravity to be the governing power.

Likewise, according to the law of value, commodities exchange for each other in proportion to the amount of socially necessary labor embodied in them respectively.

But the capitalistic wind of "supply and demand," ranging from a breeze in ordinary times to a tornado in a crisis, disturbs the proportion according to its strength.

Yet the law of value asserts itself, chiefly through the rise and fall of prices, which in economics correspond to the oscillations of the pendulum in physics.

If the swing of the market is less regular than that of the pendulum, it is because of the many capitalistic disturbances besides the so-called "law of supply and demand."

"Were our statistics as honest and perfect as the data upon which the astronomer makes his calculations, every change of value, normal or abnormal — that is resulting from some change in the method of production, in the means of transportation, in the availability of material, etc., on the one hand, could be traced to its source or sources, despite the complexity of the capitalist machine, the multiplicity and variability of the disturbing forces inherent to or evolved by capital itself, we would find the law of exchange value supreme." — Lucien Sanial in "Value, Price and Profit."

Section 2. The medium of circulation.

a. The metamorphoses of commodities.

167. We saw in a former chapter that the exchange of commodities implies contradictory and mutually exclusive conditions.

The differentiation of commodities into commodities and money does not sweep away these inconsistencies.

What does it accomplish? It develops a form by which they can exist side by side.

This is generally the way in which real contradictions are reconciled.

For instance, it is a contradiction to depict one body as constantly falling toward another, and as, at the same time, constantly flying away from it.

The ellipse is a form of motion which, while allowing this contradiction to go on, at the same time reconciles it.

168. What is the exchange process by which commodities are transferable from hands in which they are non-use-values to hands in which they become use-values? It is a social circulation of matter.

What happens to a commodity when it finds a resting place where it can serve as a use-value? It falls out of the sphere of circulation into that of consumption.

But the former sphere alone interests us at present.

We have, therefore, to consider exchange from a formal point of view; to investigate the change of form, or metamorphosis, of commodities which effectuate the social circulation of matter.

169. The comprehension of this form is, as a rule, very imperfect.

What is the cause of this imperfection? Apart from the distinct notion of value itself, every change of form in a commodity results from the exchange of two commodities, an ordinary one and the money commodity.

If we keep in view the material fact alone that a commodity has been exchanged for gold, what do we overlook? The very thing we should observe, namely, what has happened to the form of the commodity.

We overlook the fact that gold, when a mere commodity, is not money, and that, when other commodities express their prices in gold, this gold is but the money-form of these commodities themselves.

170. How does commodities first enter the process of exchange? Just as they are, articles of use.

What differentiates them into commodities and money? The process of exchange.

What does this produce? An external opposition corresponding to the internal opposition inherent in them, namely, as being at once use-values and values.

How do commodities, as use-values, stand to money? Opposed to money as exchange-value.

On the other hand, how do they stand? Both opposing sides are commodities, unities of use-value and value.

How does this unity of differences manifest itself? At two opposite poles, and at each pole in an opposite way.

Being poles they are as necessary as they are opposite.

What have we on one side of the equation? An ordinary commodity, which is, in reality a use-value.

Its value is expressed only ideally in its price, by which it is equated to its opponent, the gold, as the real embodiment of its value.

On the other hand, how does gold, in its metallic reality, rank? As the embodiment of value—as value. Gold, as gold, is exchange-value itself.

How is gold as regard to use-value? The use-value of gold has only an ideal existence, represented by the series of expressions of relative value in which it stands face to face with all other commodities, the sum of whose use makes up the sum of the various uses of gold

What are these antagonistic forms of commodities? They are the real forms in which the process of their exchange moves and takes place.

171. Let us now accompany the owner of some commodity—say our old friend the weaver—to the scene of action—the market.

His twenty yards of linen has a definite price £2. He exchanges it for the £2, and then, like a man of the good old stamp that he is, he parts with the £2, for a family bible of the same price.

The linen, which in his eyes is a mere commodity, a depository of value, he alienates in exchange for gold, which is the linen's value-form, and this form he again parts with for another commodity, the bible, which is destined to enter his house as an object of utility, and an edification to its inmates. The exchange becomes an accomplished fact by two metamorphoses of opposite yet supplementary character—the conversion of the commodity into money, and the re-conversion of the money into a commodity. The two phases of this metamorphosis are both of them distinct transactions of the weaver, selling or the exchange of a commodity for money; buying or the exchange of money for a commodity; and, the unity of these two acts, selling in order to buy.

172. What is the result of the whole transaction? This: as regards the weaver, that, instead of being in possession of the linen, he now has the bible; instead of his original commodity, he now possesses another of the same value, but of different utilities.

In like manner he procures his other means of subsistence and means of production.

What has the whole process effected from his point of view? Nothing more than the exchange of the product of his labor for the product of someone's else, nothing more than the exchange of products.

What are the exchange of commodities accompanied by? The following change in their form: Commodity — money — commodity.

What is the result of the process so far as it concerns the objects? C—C, the exchange of one commodity for another, the circulation of materialized social labor, when this result is attained the process is at an end.

C — M. First metamorphosis or sale.

174. The leap taken by value from the body of the commodity into the body of the gold is, as I have elsewhere called it, the mortal leap of the commodity.

If it falls short, then, although the commodity itself is not hurt, its owner decidedly is.

What does the social division of labor cause his labor to be? As one sided as his wants are many sided.

What is the reason that the product of his labor serves him solely as exchange-value? For the reason that his labor is one-sided.

How can his labor acquire, for him, the property of a socially recognized universal equivalent? Only by its being converted into money.

That money, however, is in someone's else pocket. What must our friend's commodity be in order to entice the money out of that pocket? A use-value for the owner of the money.

For this it is necessary that the labor spent upon it be of a kind that is socially useful — of a kind that constitutes a branch of the social division of labor.

How has this system of production, which must have the social division of labor, grown up? Spontaneously, and continues to grow behind the backs of the producers.

The commodity to be exchanged may possibly be the product of some new kind of labor that pretends to satisfy some newly arisen requirement, or even give rise itself to new requirements.

A particular operation, though yesterday, perhaps, forming one out of the many operations conducted by one producer in creating a given commodity, may today separate itself from this connection; may establish itself as an independent branch of labor and send its incomplete product to market as an independent commodity.

The circumstances may or may not be ripe for such a separation.

Today the product may satisfy a social want, tomorrow the article may, either altogether or partly, be superceded by some other more appropriate product.

Moreover, although our weaver's labor may be a recognized branch of the social division of labor, yet that fact is by no means sufficient to guarantee the utility of his 20 yards of linen.

If the community's want of linen—and such a want has a limit, like every other want—should already be saturated by the product of rival weavers, our friend's product is superfluous, redundant, and consequently useless.

Although people do not look a gift horse in the mouth, our friend does not frequent the market for the purpose of making presents.

But, suppose his product turn out a real use-value and thereby attract money?

The question arises, how much will it attract?

No doubt the answer is anticipated in the price of the article, in the exponent of the magnitude of value.

We leave out of consideration here any accidental miscalculation on the value by our friend—a mistake that is soon rectified in the market.

We suppose him to have spent on his product only that amount of labor-time that is, on an average, socially necessary.

The price, then, is merely the money-name of the quantity of social labor realized in his commodity.

But, without leave, and behind the back, of our weaver, the old-fashioned mode of weaving undergoes a change.

The labor-time that yesterday was, without doubt, socially necessary to the production of a yard of linen, ceases to be so today—a fact which the owner of the money is only too eager to prove from the prices quoted by our friend's competitors.

Unluckily for him weavers are not few and far between.

Lastly, suppose that every piece of linen in the market contains no more labor-time than is socially necessary. In spite of this, all the pieces, taken as a whole, may have had superfluous labor-time spent upon them.

NOTE — If 1,000 yards of linen was sufficient to satisfy the want of society, for linen, and one hour was the labor-time socially necessary to produce one yard of linen, then 1,000 yards would be the necessary amount of linen, and 1,000 hours labor-time the value of the linen.

But if, from insufficient knowledge of the need of society, we were to spend 1,500 hours of social labor-time and produce 1,500 yards of linen, we would be wasting 500 hours of labor-time — for that amount of time would be spent on something useless — and would not count as labor, nor would it create any value.

The labor-time socially necessary to produce the necessary quantity being 1,000 hours, the 1,500 yards of linen would contain only 1,000 hours labor-time, and one yard would have the value of one-fifteen-hundreth part of 1,000 hours labor-time value, or the value of 40 minutes necessary labor-time.

If the market cannot stomach the whole quantity at the normal price of 2 shillings a yard, this proves that too great a portion of the total labor-time of the community had been expended in weaving.

The effect is the same as if each individual weaver had expended more labor-time upon his particular product than was socially necessary.

Here we may say, with the German proverb "Caught together, hung together." All the linen in the market counts but as one article of commerce, of which each piece is only an aliquot part.

And, as a matter of fact, the value of each single yard is but the materialized form of the same definite and socially fixed quantity of homogeneous human labor.

174. We see, then, commodities are in love with money; but, "the course of true love never did run smooth."

How is the quantitative division of labor brought about? In the same spontaneous and accidental manner as its qualitative division.

What do the owners of commodities find out? That the same division of labor that turns them into private producers also frees the social process of production and the relation of the individual producers to each other within that process from all dependence on the will of the producers, and that the seeming mutual independence of the individuals is supplemented by a system of mutual dependence through and by means of the product.

175. The division of labor converts the product into a commodity, and thereby makes necessary its further conversion into money.

At the same time it makes the accomplishment of this transubstantiation quite accidental.

Here, however, we are only concerned with the phenomena in its integrity, that is, if the commodity be not absolutely unsaleable its metamorphosis does take place although the price realized may be abnormally above or below its value.

176. The seller has his commodity replaced by gold, the buyer has his gold replaced by a commodity.

What fact here stares us in the face? That a commodity and gold, twenty yards of linen and £2, have changed hands and places; in other words, they have been exchanged.

For what is the commodity exchanged? For the shape assumed by its own value; for the universal equivalent.

And for what is the gold exchanged? For a particular form of its own use-value.

Why does gold take the form of money face to face with the linen? Because the linen's price of £2, its denomination in money, has already equated the linen to gold in its character of money.

When does a commodity strip off its original commodity-form? On the instant its use-value actually attracts gold, that before existed only ideally in its price.

The realization of a commodity's price, or of its ideal value-form, is therefore at the same time the realization of the use-value of money; the conversion of a commodity into money is the simultaneous conversion of money into a commodity.

The apparently single process is in reality a double one.

From the pole of a commodity owner it is a sale, from the opposite pole of the money owner it is a purchase.

177. Till now, how have we considered men? Only in one economic capacity, that of owners of commodities; a capacity in which they appropriate the products of the labor of others by alienating that of their own.

What is necessary for one commodity owner to meet with another that has money? Either that the product of the buyer should be money — gold, the material of which money consists — or that it should already have changed its skin, and have stripped off its original form of a useful object.

What must gold do in order to play the part of money? Enter the market at some point or another.

Where is this point to be found? At the source of the production of the metal — at the mines.

What happens to the gold at this point? It is bartered, as the immediate product of labor, for some other product of equal value.

NOTE — In the United States, the bullion is exchanged at the mint for coined money, except from small miners. This is what is termed free coinage. The mint assays the bullion and give in return as much coin as the bullion equals in fineness and weight.

And what does it represent? From that moment it always represents the realized price of some commodity.

Apart from its exchange for other commodities at the source of its production, gold, in whosesoever hands, is the transformed shape of some commodity alienated by its owner; it is the product of a sale or the first metamorphosis, C — M.

How did gold become the ideal money, or a measure of value? It became so in consequence of all commodities measuring their values by it, and thus contrasting it ideally with their natural shapes as useful objects, and making it the shape of their value.

How did gold become the real money? By the general alienation of commodities, by actually changing places with their natural forms as useful objects, and thus becoming in reality the embodiment of their values.

What do commodities assume, when they strip off every trace of their natural use-values? They assume the money-shape, when they strip off their natural use-value, and of the particular kind of labor to which they owe their existence, in order to transform themselves into the uniform socially recognized incarnation of homogeneous human labor.

Under the money-form all commodities look alike. Hence money may be dirt, although dirt is not money.

We will assume that the two pieces in consideration of which our weaver has parted with his linen are the metamorphosed shape of a quarter of wheat.

The sale of the linen C−M, is at the same time its purchase, M−C.

But, the sale is the first act of a process that ends with a transaction of an opposite nature−namely, the purchase of a bible; the purchase of the linen, on the other hand, ends a movement that began with a transaction of an opposite nature, namely, with the sale of the wheat. C-M. (linen and money) which is the first phase of C−M−C (linen−money−bible) is also M−C (money−linen) the last phase of another movement, C−M−C (wheat−money−linen).

The first metamorphosis of one commodity, its transformation from a commodity into money, is therefore also invariably the second metamorphosis of some other commodity, the transformation of the latter from money into a commodity.

M−C, or purchase the second and concluding metamorphosis of a commodity.

178. For what reason is money alienable without restriction or condition? Because it is the metamorphosed shape of all other commodities, the result of their general alienation.

How does money read prices? Backwards, and thus depicts itself in the bodies of all commodities that offer to it the material for the realization of its own use-value.

How does price define the limit of the convertibility of money? By pointing to its quantity.

Since every commodity, on becoming money, disappears as a commodity, it is impossible to tell from the money itself, how it got into the hands of its possessor, or what article has been exchanged for it.

No matter from whatever source it may come.

Representing, on the one hand, a sold commodity, it represents on the other a commodity to be bought.

179. M−C, a purchase is at the same time C−M, a sale; the concluding metamorphosis of one commodity is the first metamorphosis of another.

With regard to our weaver, the life of his commodity ends with the bible, into which he has converted his £2.

But suppose the seller of the bible turns the £2 set free by the weaver into brandy, M−C, the concluding phase of C−M−C (linen, money, bible), is also C−M, the first phase of C−M−C (bible, money, brandy).

The producer of a particular commodity has that one article alone to offer; this he sells, very often, in large quantities, but his many and various wants compel him to split up the price realized, the sum of money set free, into numerous purchases.

Hence a sale leads to many purchases of various articles.

The concluding metamorphosis of a commodity thus constitutes an aggregation of first metamorphosis of various other commodities.

180. If we consider the complete metamorphosis of a commodity, as a whole, how does it appear? In the first place, it appears that it is made up of two opposite and complementary movements C−M and M−C.

How are these two antithetical transmutations brought about? By two antithetical social acts on the part of the owner.

And these acts in their turn stamp the character of the economical parts played by him.

As a person who makes a sale he is a seller; as a person who makes a purchase he is a buyer.

But, just as upon every transmutation of a commodity its two forms, commodity-form, and money-form, exist simultaneously, but at two different poles, so every seller has a buyer opposed to him and every buyer a seller.

While one commodity is going through its two transmutations in succession, from commodity into money and from money into another commodity, the owner changes in succession his part from that of seller to that of buyer.

These characters of seller and buyer are, therefore, not permanent, but attach themselves in turn to the various persons engaged in the circulation of commodities.

181. What does the complete metamorphosis of a commodity, in its simplest form, imply? Four extremes and three *dramatis persona* (dramatical characters).

First a commodity comes face to face with money; money is the form taken by the commodity, and exists in all its hard reality in the pocket of the buyer.

A commodity owner is thus brought into contact with the possessor of money.

So soon now as the commodity has been changed into money, the money becomes its transient equivalent form, the use-value of which equivalent is to be found in the bodies of other commodities.

Money, the final term of the first transmutation, is at the same time the starting point for the second.

The person who is seller in the first transaction, becomes a buyer in the second, in which a third commodity owner appears on the scene as a seller.

182. What do the two phases, each inverse to the other, that make up the metamorphoses of a commodity constitute? A circular movement, a circuit; commodity form, stripping off of this form, and returning to the commodity-form.

How does the commodity here appear? Under two different aspects, at the starting point it is not a use-value to its owner, at the finishing point it is.

How does money appear in the first phase? As a solid crystal of value, a crystal into which the commodity eagerly solidifies.

How does it appear in the second phase? To dissolve into the mere transient equivalent form destined to be replace by a use-value.

183. The two metamorphoses constituting the circuit are at the same time two inverse partial metamorphoses of two other commodities.

One and the same commodity, the linen, opens the series of its own metamorphoses, and completes the metamorphosis of another, the wheat.

In the first phase or sale the linen plays these two parts in its own person.

But, then, changed into gold, it completes its own second and final metamorphosis, and helps at the same time to accomplish the first metamorphosis of a third commodity.

Hence the circuit made by one commodity in the course of its metamorphoses is inextricably mixed up with the circuits of other commodities.

What does the total of all the different circuits constitute? The circulation of commodities.

184. Does the circulation of commodities differ from the direct exchange of products, that is, barter? Not only in form but also in substance. Only consider the course of events.

The weaver has, as a matter of fact, exchanged his linen for a bible, his commodity for someone's else.

But this is true only so far as he himself is concerned.

The seller of the bible, who prefers something to warm his insides, no more thought of exchanging his bible for linen than our weaver knew that wheat had been exchanged for his linen.

B's commodity replaces that of A, but A and B do not mutually exchange those commodities.

It may, of course, happen, that A and B make simultaneous purchases; the one from the other, but such exceptional transactions are by no means the necessary result of the general condition of the circulation of commodities.

We see here, on the one hand, how the exchange of commodities break through all local and personal bonds inseparable from direct barter, and develops the circulation of the products of social labor; on the other hand, how it develops a whole net work of social relations spontaneous in their growth and entirely beyond the control of the actors.

It is only because the farmer has sold his wheat that the weaver is enabled to sell his linen; only because our weaver has sold his linen our "Hotspur" is enabled to sell his bible; and only because the latter has sold the water of everlasting life that the distiller is enabled to sell his *eau-de-vie* (brandy), and so on.

185. The process of circulation, therefore, does not, like direct barter of products, become extinguished upon the use-value exchanging place and hands.

The money does not vanish on dropping out of the circuit of the metamorphosis of a given commodity.

It is constantly being precipitated into new places in the arena of circulation vacated by other commodities.

In the complete metamorphosis of the linen, for example, linen — money — bible, the linen first falls out of circulation, and money steps into its place.

When one commodity replaces another, the money always sticks to the hand of some third person.

Circulation sweats money from every pore.

Bear this well in mind, as it covers that oft mistaken notion that commodities are sold readily, when money is plenty, whereas money has a rapid currency when commodities has a rapid circulation.

186. Nothing can be more childish than the dogma that, because every sale is a purchase, and every purchase a sale, therefore the circulation of commodities necessarily implies an equilibrium of sales and purchases.

If this means that the actual sales is equal to the number of purchases, it is merely tautology.

But its real purpose is to prove that every seller brings his buyer to market with him; nothing of the kind.

The sale and the purchase constitute one identical act—an exchange between a commodity owner and an owner of money, between two persons as opposite to each other, as the two poles of a magnet. They form two distinct acts, of polar and opposite character; when performed by one single person.

What does the identity of sale and purchase imply? That the commodity is useless, if on being thrown into the alchemistical retort of circulation it does not come out again in the shape of money; in other words, if it cannot be sold by its owner, and therefore be bought by the owner of the money.

What does this identity further imply? That exchange, if it does take place, constitutes a period of rest—an interval long or short in the life of the commodity. Since the first metamorphosis of a commodity is at once a sale and a purchase, it is also an independent process in itself.

The purchaser has a commodity, the seller has the money; that is, a commodity ready to go into circulation at any time. No one can sell unless some one else purchases. But no one is forthwith bound to purchase because he has just sold.

What does this show us? That circulation bursts through all restrictions as to time, place, and individuals imposed by direct barter.

How is this effected? By splitting up, into the antithesis of a sale and a purchase, the direct identity that does exist between the alienation of one's own and the acquisition of some other man's product.

To say that these two independent and antithetical acts have an intrinsic unity—are essentially one—is the same as to say that this intrinsic oneness expresses itself in an external antithesis.

If the interval of time between the two complementary phases of the complete metamorphoses of a commodity become too great—if the split between sale and purchase become too pronounced—the intimate connection between them, their oneness, asserts itself, what is produced? A crisis—that is, if more goods are produced than both the home and foreign markets can purchase, production must cease, and this results in throwing large numbers out of employment which destroys the purchasing power of the home market, both home and foreign market being unable to purchase, a crisis is the result.

The antithesis, use-value and value, the contradiction that private labor is bound to manifest itself as direct social labor; the contradiction between the personification of objects and representation of persons by things—all these antithesis and contradictions, which are imminent in commodities assert themselves and develop their mode of motion in the antithetical phases of the metamorphoses of a commodity.

These modes, therefore, imply the possibility, and no more than the possibility, of crises. The conversion of this possibility into a reality is the result of a long series of relations that, from our standpoint of the simple circulation of commodities, have as yet no existence.

b. The currency of money.

187. What is required for the change of form C-M-C by which the circulation of the material products of labor is brought about? That a given value in the shape of a commodity shall begin the process, and shall also, in the shape of a commodity, end it.

What is this movement of a commodity? A circuit.

On the other hand, how does this circuit affect the money? It precludes the money from making a circuit.

What is the result? Not the return of the money, but its continual removal further and further away from the starting point.

So long as the seller sticks fast to his money, which is the transformed shape of his commodity, that commodity is still in the first phase of its metamorphosis, and has completed only half its course.

But, so soon as he completes the process, so soon as he supplements his sale by a purchase, the money again leaves the hands of its possessor.

It is true, if the weaver, after buying the bible, sells more, money comes back into his hands.

But this return is not owing to the circulation of the first twenty yards of linen; that circulation resulted in the money getting into the hands of the seller of the bible.

The return of the money into the hands of the weaver is brought about only by the renewal or repetition of the process of circulation with a fresh commodity, which renewed process ends with the same result as its predecessor did.

Hence the movement directly imparted to the money by the circulation of commodities, takes the form of a constant motion away from its starting point — of a course from the hands of one commodity owner to those of another.

This course constitutes its currency.

188. The currency of money is the constant and monotonous repetition of the same process. The commodity is always in the hands of the seller; the money, as a means of purchase, always in the hands of the buyer.

And money serves as a means of purchase by realizing the price of the commodity.

This realization transfers the commodity from the seller to the buyer, and removes the money from the hands of the buyer into those of the seller, where it again goes through the same process with another commodity. That this one-sided character of the money's motion arises out of the two-sided character of the commodity's motion is a circumstance that is veiled over.

The very nature of the circulation of commodities begets the opposite appearance. In the first metamorphosis of a commodity is visibly not only the money's movement, but also that of the commodity itself; in the second metamorphosis, on the contrary, the movement appears to us as the movement of the money alone.

In the first phase of its circulation the commodity changes place with the money. Thereupon the commodity, under its aspect as a useful object, falls out of circulation into that of consumption, in its stead we have its value-shape — money.

It then goes through its second phase of circulation, but under the shape of money.

The continuity of this movement is, therefore, kept up by the money alone; and the same movement as regards the commodity consists of two processes of an antithetical character, is when considered as the movement of the money, always one and the same process—a continual change of places with ever fresh commodities.

Hence the result brought about by the circulation of commodities, namely, the replacing of one commodity by another, takes the appearance of having been effected, not by means of the change of form of the commodities, but rather as the money acting as a medium of circulation, by an action that circulates commodities, to all appearances motionless in themselves, and transfers them from hands in which they are non-use-values to hands in which they are use-values; and that in a direction continually drawing commodities from circulation and stepping into their place, and in this way continually moving further and further from its starting point.

What appearance has the movement of the money? Although its movement is merely the expression of the circulation of commodities, yet the contrary appears to be the actual fact, and the circulation of commodities seems to be the result of the movement of the money.

189. Why does money function as the means of circulation? Only because in it the value of commodities have independent reality.

What is its movement, as the means of circulation? Merely the movement of commodities while changing their form.

How does this fact make itself visible? In the currency of money.

How is the two-fold change in the form of a commodity reflected? In the twice repeated change of place of the same piece of money during the complete metamorphosis of a commodity and in its constantly repeated change of place, as metamorphosis follow metamorphosis and each becomes interlaced with the other.

190. The linen, for instance, first of all changes its commodity-form for its money-form.

The last term of its first metamorphosis (C−M) , or the money-form, is the first term of its final metamorphosis (M−C), or its reconversion into a useful commodity—the bible.

But each of these changes of form is accomplished by an exchange between commodity and money, by their reciprocal displacement.

The same piece of coin in the first act changed places with the linen; in the second with the bible.

They are displaced twice.

The first metamorphosis puts them in the weaver's pocket, the second draws them out of it.

The two inverse changes undergone by the same commodity are reflected in the displacement, twice repeated, but in opposite directions, of the same piece of coin.

191. If, on the contrary, only one phase of the metamorphosis is gone through, if there are only sales, or only purchases, then a given piece of money changes its place only once.

What does this second change correspond to and express? The second metamorphosis of a commodity—its re-conversion from money into another commodity intended for use.

It is a matter of course that all this is applicable to the simple circulation of commodities alone, the only form we are now considering.

192. What happens to a commodity when its first steps into circulation and undergoes its first change of form? It falls out of circulation and is replaced by another commodity.

What happens to money, as a medium of circulation? It keeps continually within the sphere of circulation and moves about in it.

The question, therefore, arises, how much money this sphere constantly absorbs.

193. In a given country there takes place every day, at the same time, but in different localities, numerous one sided metamorphosis of commodities, or in other words, numerous sales and numerous purchases.

The commodities are equated beforehand in imagination by their prices, to definite quantities of money.

And since, in the form of circulation now under consideration, money and commodities come bodily face to face, one at the positive pole of purchase, the other at the negative pole of sale; it is clear that the amount of the means of circulation required is determined beforehand by the sum of the prices of all these commodities.

As a matter of fact, the money in reality represents the quantity or sum of gold ideally expressed by the sum of the prices of the commodities.

The quantity of these two sums is, therefore, self-evident.

We know, however, that the value of commodities remaining constant, their prices vary with the value of gold (the material of money) rising in proportion as it falls, and falling in proportion as it rises.

Now if, in consequence of such a rise or fall in the value of gold, the sum of the prices fall or rise, the sum of money in currency must fall or rise to the same extent.

What is this change of quantity of the circulating medium caused by? In this case, by money itself, not in virtue of its function as a circulating medium, but of its function as a measure of value.

What would the result be if we were to change the material of the circulating medium from gold to silver, or vice versa? First, the price of the commodities vary inversely as the value of the money, then the quantity of the circulating medium varies directly as the price of the commodities.

Exactly the same thing would happen if, for instance, instead of the value of gold falling, gold were replaced by silver as a measure of value, or if, instead of the value of silver rising, gold were to thrust silver out from being the measure of value.

In the one case more silver would be current than gold was before; in the other case, less gold would be current than silver was before.

In each case the value of the material of money, that is the value of the commodity that serves as the measure of value, would have undergone a change, and therefore, so, too, would the prices of commodities which express their value in money, and so, too, would the quantity of money current whose function it is to realize those prices.

We have already seen that the sphere of circulation has an opening through which gold (or the material of money generally) enters into it as a commodity with a given value.

Hence, when money enters on its function as a measure of value, when it expresses prices, its value is already determined.

If now the value of money falls, how is the fact first made evident? By a change in the price of those commodities that are directly bartered for the precious metals at the source of their production.

In the imperfectly developed stage of civil society, the greater part of all other commodities will continue for a long time to be estimated by the antiquated illusory value of the measure of value.

Nevertheless one commodity infects another through their common value relation, so that their prices, in gold or in silver, gradually settle down into the proportion determined by their comparative values until finally the value of all commodities are estimated in the new value of the metal that constitutes money.

What causes increased quantities of the precious metals to enter this process? Their streaming in to replace the articles bartered for them at the place of their production.

In proportion, therefore, as commodities acquire their true prices, in proportion as their values become estimated according to the fallen value of the precious metals, in the same proportion the quantity of that metal necessary for realizing those new prices is provided beforehand.

A one sided observation of the results that followed upon the discovery of fresh supplies of gold and silver led some economists in the seventeenth century, and particularly in the eighteenth century, to the false conclusion that the prices of commodities had gone up in consequence of the increased quantity of gold and silver serving as means of circulation.

Henceforth, we shall consider the value of gold to be given, as, in fact, it is momentarily whenever we estimate the price of a commodity.

194. On this supposition, then, how is the quantity of the medium of circulation determined? By the sum of the prices to be realized.

If, now, we further suppose the price of each commodity to be given, upon what does the sum of the prices depend? Clearly, upon the mass of commodities in circulation.

It requires little wracking of brains to comprehend that if one quarter of wheat cost $10, 100 quarters of wheat will cost $1,000, 200 quarters $2,000, and so on; that, consequently, the quantity of money that changes places with the wheat, when sold, must increase with the quantity of the wheat.

195. If the mass of commodities remain constant, how does the quantity of circulating money vary? With the fluctuations in the prices of those commodities.

Why? Because the sum of the prices increases or diminishes in consequence of the change in price.

To produce this effect must the price of all commodities rise or fall simultaneously? By no means. A rise or fall in the price of a number of leading articles is sufficient to increase or diminish the sum of the prices of all commodities, and, therefore, to put more or less money in circulation.

Whether the change in the prices corresponds to an actual change of value in the commodities, or whether it be the result of a mere fluctuation in the market prices, the effect on the quantity of the medium of circulation remains the same.

196. Suppose the following articles to be sold or partially metamorphosed simultaneously in different localities; say one quarter of wheat, 20 yards of linen, one bible, and four gallons of brandy.

If the price of each article be $2, and the sum of the prices to be realized be consequently $8, it follows that $8 in money must go into circulation.

If on the other hand, these same articles are links in the chain of metamorphoses, one quarter of wheat $2 — 20 yards of linen $2 — one bible $2 — four gallons of brandy $2, a chain that is already well known to us, in that case the $2 causes the different commodities to circulate one after the other, and after realizing their prices successively, and, therefore, the sum of those prices $8, they come to rest at last in the pocket of the distiller.

The $2 thus makes four moves.

To what does this repeated change of place of the same pieces of money correspond? To the double change in the form of the commodities, to their motion in opposite directions through two stages of circulation, and to the interlacing of the metamorphoses of different commodities.

These antithetical and complementary phases, of which the process of metamorphoses consists, are gone through, not simultaneously but successively.

Time is therefore required for the completion of the series.

How do we measure the velocity of the currency of money?

By the number of moves made by a given piece of money in a given time.

Suppose the circulation of the four articles takes a day.

The sum of the prices to be realized in the day is $8, the number of moves of the two pieces of money is four, and the quantity of money circulating is $2.

Hence for a given interval of time during the process of circulation, what is the quantity of money functioning as the circulating medium? The quantity of circulating medium is equal to the sum of the prices of the commodities divided by the number of moves made by coins of the same denomination.

This law holds good generally.

197. The total circulation of commodities in a given country during a given period is made up, on the one hand, of numerous isolated and simultaneously partial metamorphoses—sales which are at the same time purchases, in which each coin changes its place only once, or makes only one move; on the other hand, of numerous distinct series of metamorphoses running side by side, and partly coalescing with each other, in each of which series each coin makes a number of moves, the number being greater or less according to circumstances.

How do we determine the average velocity of the currency of money? The total number of moves made by all the circulating coins of one denomination being given, we can arrive at the average number of moves made by a single coin of that denomination, or at the average velocity of the currency of money.

Since the quantity of money capable of being absorbed by the circulation is given for a given mean velocity of currency, all that is necessary in order to abstract a given number of dollars from the circulation is to throw the same number of one dollar notes into it—a trick well-known to all bankers.

198. Just as the currency of money, generally considered, is but a reflex of the circulation of commodities, or of the antithetical metamorphoses they undergo, so too, the velocity of the currency reflects the rapidity with which commodities change their forms, the continual interlacing of one series of metamorphoses with another, the hurried social interchange of matter, the rapid disappearance of commodities from the sphere of circulation, and the equally rapid substitution of fresh ones in their place.

NOTE—The oft mistaken notion that money is plentiful or scarce according as the circulation of commodities are rapid or sluggish is here shown to be the reverse, that when the circulation of commodities are brisk, money seems to be plenty, because a larger quantity is in currency.

When the circulation of commodities are sluggish, money seems to be scarce because it is in hoarding.

Does the money vanish during a crisis? Certainly not. It becomes hoarded in the banks.

When "prosperity" booms, does the money materialize again? Certainly not. It flows out of hoarding to be used in the circulation of commodities.

Money increases when more gold is mined and sent to the mint and coined. It diminishes when foreign trade is brisk and we have to pay a large balance. Or when foreign capital, invested in this country, draws its dividends.

Hence, in the velocity of currency, the fluent unity of the antithetical and complementary phases, the unity, of the conversion of the useful aspect of commodities into their value aspect, and their re-conversion from the latter aspect to the former, or the unity of the two phases, sale and purchase.

On the other hand, the retardation of the currency reflects the separation of these two processes into isolated antithetical phases, reflects the stagnation in the change in form, and, therefore, in the social interchange of matter.

The circulation itself, of course, gives no clue to the origin of this stagnation; it merely puts in evidence the phenomenon itself.

The general public, who, simultaneously with the retardation of the circulation, see money appear and disappear at the periphery of circulation, naturally attribute this retardation to the deficiency in the circulating medium.

199. How is the total quantity of money functioning, during a given period, as the circulating medium determined? On the one hand, by the prices of the circulating commodities; on the other hand, by the rapidity with which the antithetical phases of the metamorphosis follow one another.

What depends upon this rapidity? What proportion of the sum of the prices can, on an average, be realized by each single coin.

What does the sum of the prices of the circulating commodities depend? The quantity as well as the prices of the commodities.

These three factors, however, state of prices, quantity of circulating commodities, velocity of currency, are all variable.

Hence, the sum of the prices to be realized, and consequently the quantity of the circulating medium depending on that sum, will vary with the numerous variations of these three factors in combination.

Of these variations we shall consider those alone that have been the most important in the history of prices.

200. Prices remaining constant, how may the quantity of circulating medium increase? Owing to the number of circulating commodities increasing, or to the velocity of currency decreasing, or to a combination of the two.

How may it decrease, prices remaining the same? Owing to a decrease of the number of circulating commodities, or with an increasing rapidity of their circulation.

201. How may the quantity of circulating medium remain constant, with a general rise in the prices of commodities? Provided that the number of commodities in circulation decrease proportionately to the increase in the price, or provided that the velocity of the currency increases at the same rate as the prices rise, the number of commodities remaining the same.

How may the quantity of circulating medium decrease, prices remaining the same? Owing to the number of commodities decreasing more rapidly; or to the currency increasing more rapidly than prices rise.

202. How may the quantity of the circulating medium remain constant, with a general fall in the prices of commodities? Provided the number of commodities increase proportionately to their fall in prices, or provided the velocity of currency decrease in the same proportion.

How may the quantity of circulating medium increase, with a general fall in prices? Provided the number of commodities increase faster; or the rapidity of circulation decrease faster than the prices fall.

203. The variation of the different factors may compensate each other, so that, notwithstanding their instability, the sum of the prices to be realized and the quantity of money in circulation remains constant; consequently, we find, especially if we take long periods

into consideration, that the deviation from the average level, of the quantity of money current in any country, are much smaller than we should at first sight expect, apart, of course, from excessive perturbations periodically arising from industrial crises, less frequently from the fluctuation in the value of money.

204. The law that the quantity of circulating medium is determined by the sum of the prices of the commodities circulating, and the average velocity of currency, may also be stated as follows: Given the sum of the values of commodities, and the average rapidity of their metamorphoses, the quantity of precious metal current as money depends on the value of the precious metal.

The erroneous opinion that it is, on the contrary, prices that are determined by the quantity of circulating medium, and that the latter depends on the quantity of precious metal in a country; this opinion was based by those who first held it upon the absurd hypothesis that commodities are without a price, and money without a value, when they first enter into circulation, and, that once in the circulation, an aliquot part of the medley of commodities is exchanged for an aliquot part of the heap of precious metals.

c. Coin and symbols of value.

What does coin, the shape that money takes, spring from? From its function as the circulating medium.

The weight of gold represented in imagination by the prices, or money names, of commodities, must confront these commodities, in the shape of coin, or pieces of gold, of a given denomination.

Coining, like the establishment of the standard of prices, is the business of the State.

The different national uniforms worn at home by gold and silver coin, and doffed again in the markets of the world, indicate the separation between the internal or national spheres of the circulation of commodities and their universal spheres.

205. What is the difference between coin and bullion? Only the shape, and gold can, at any time, pass from one to the other.

For, no sooner does gold leave the mint than it finds itself on the high road to the melting pot.

During their currency, coins wear away, some more others less.

Name and substance, normal weight and real weight, begin their separation, coins of the same denomination become different in value because they are different in weight.

The weight of gold fixed upon as the standard of prices deviates from the weight that serves as the circulating medium, and the latter thereby ceases to be a real equivalent for the commodity whose price it realizes.

The history of coinage during the middle ages and down into the eighteenth century records the ever renewed confusion arising from this cause.

A natural tendency to convert coins into a mere semblance of what they profess to be, into the symbol of the weight of metal they are officially supposed to contain, is recognized by modern legislation, which fixes the loss of weight sufficient to demonetize a gold coin, or to make it no longer legal tender.

206. The fact that the currency of coin itself effects a separation between them as mere pieces of metal on the one hand, and as coins with a definite function on the other, imply what? The latent possibility of replacing metallic coins by tokens of some other material, by symbols serving the same purpose as coins.

The practical difficulty in the way of coining extremely minute quantities of gold and silver, and circumstances that at first the less precious metal is used as a measure of value instead of the more precious, copper instead of silver, silver instead of gold, and that the less precious circulates as money until dethroned by the more precious—all these facts explain the parts historically played by silver and copper tokens as substitutes for gold coins.

Where do silver and copper tokens take the place of gold? In those regions of circulation where coins pass from hand to hand most rapidly, and are subject to the maximum amount of wear and tear.

This occurs where sales and purchases on a very small scale are continually happening.

In order to prevent the satellites from establishing themselves permanently in the place of gold, positive enactments determine the extent to which they must be compulsory received as payments instead of gold.

The particular tracks pursued by the different species of coin in currency run mutually into each other.

The tokens keep company with gold, to pay fractional parts of the smallest gold coins; gold is, on the one hand, constantly pouring into retail circulation, and, on the other hand, is constantly being thrown out again by being changed into tokens.

207. The weight of metal in silver and copper tokens is arbitrarily fixed by law.

When in currency, they wear away even more rapidly than gold coins.

Hence, their functions are totally independent of their weight, and consequently of all value.

The function of gold as coin becomes completely independent of the metallic value of the gold.

Therefore things that are relatively without value, such as paper notes, can serve as coins in its place.

This purely symbolical character is, to a certain extent, masked in metal tokens, in paper money it stands out plainly. In fact, it is only the first step that is difficult.

208. We refer here only to inconvertible paper money issued by the state, and having compulsory circulation.

Money based upon credit implies, on the other hand, contradictions, which, from our standpoint of simple circulation of commodities, are as yet totally unknown to us.

But, we may affirm this much, that just as true paper money takes its rise in the function of money as the circulating medium, so money based upon credit takes root spontaneously in the function of money as means of payment.

209. The state puts into circulation bits of paper on which the various denominations — say $1.00, $5.00 — are printed.

In so far as they actually take the place of gold, to the same amount, their movement is subject to the laws that regulate the currency of money itself.

A law peculiar to the circulation of paper money can spring up only from the proportion in which paper money represents gold. Such a law exists; stated simply, it is as follows: The issue of paper money must not exceed the amount of gold, or silver as the case may be, which would actually circulate if not replaced by symbols.

Now the quantity of circulating medium in a given country never sinks below a certain minimum easily ascertained by actual experience.

The fact that this minimum mass continually undergoes changes in its constituent parts, or that the pieces of gold of which it consists are being constantly replaced by fresh ones, causes, of course, no change either in its amount or in the continuity of its circulation.

It can, therefore, be replaced by paper symbols.

If, on the other hand, all the conduits of circulation were today filled with paper money, to the full extent of their capacity for absorbing money, they might tomorrow be overflowing in consequence of the fluctuation in the circulation of commodities.

There would no longer be any standard.

If the paper money exceeds its proper limit, which is the amount in gold coin of the like denomination that can actually be current, it would, apart from the danger of falling into general disrepute, represent only that quantity of gold, which in accordance with the laws of the circulation of commodities, it required, and is alone capable of being represented by paper.

If the quantity of paper money issued be double the quantity which it ought to be, then, as a matter of fact, $20 would be the money name, not of one ounce but of one-half ounce of gold.

The effect would be the same as if an alteration had taken place in the function of gold as a standard of price.

Those values that were previously expressed by the $20 would now be expressed by the price of $40.

210. Paper money is a token representing gold, or money.

The relation between it and the values of commodities is this, that the latter are ideally expressed in the same quantities of gold that are symbolically represented by the paper.

Only in so far as paper money represents gold, which like all other commodities, has value in it, is it a symbol of value.

211. Finally, some one may ask why gold is capable of being replaced by tokens that have no value?

But, as we have already seen, it is capable of being replaced only in so far as it functions exclusively as coin, or as the circulating medium, and as nothing else.

Now, money has other functions besides this one, the circulating medium is not necessarily the only one attached to gold coin, although this is the case with those abraided coins that continue to circulate.

Each piece of money is a mere coin, or means of circulation, only so long as it actually circulates.

But, this is just the case with the minimum mass of gold which is capable of being replaced by paper money.

That mass remains constantly within the sphere of circulation, continually functions as a circulating medium, and exists exclusively for that purpose.

Its movement, therefore, represents nothing but the continued alteration of the inverse phases of the metamorphoses $C-M-C$, phases in which commodities confront their value-forms, only to disappear again immediately.

The independent existence of the exchange-value of a commodity is here a transient apparition, by means of which the commodity is immediately replaced by another commodity.

Hence, in this process, which continually makes money pass from hand to hand, the mere symbolical existence of money suffices.

Its functional existence absorbs, so to say, its material existence.

Being a transient and objective reflex of the price of commodities, it serves only as a symbol of itself, and is, therefore, capable of being replaced by a token.

One thing, however, is requisite: this token must have an objective social validity of its own, and this the paper symbol acquires by its forced currency.

This compulsory action of the state can take effect only within the inner sphere of circulation which is coterminous with the territory of the community; but it is also only within that sphere that money completely responds to its function of being the circulating medium, or becomes coin.

Section 3. Money.

212. The commodity that functions as a measure of value, and, either in its own person or by a representative, as the medium of circulation, is money, gold and silver is therefore money.

It functions as money, on the one hand, when it has to be present in its golden person. It is then the money commodity — neither merely ideal, as in its function as a measure of value, nor capable of being represented, as in its function as a circulating medium.

On the other hand, it also functions as money when, by virtue of its function, whether that function be performed in person or by a representative, it congeals into the sole form of value, the only adequate form of existence of exchange-value, in opposition to use-value, represented by all other commodities.

a. Hoarding.

213. The continual movement in circuits of the two antithetical metamorphoses of commodities, or the never ceasing alteration of sale and purchase, is reflected in the restless currency of money or in the function that money performs of a perpetual motion of circulation.

But so soon as the metamorphosis is interrupted, so soon as sales are not supplemented by subsequent purchases, money ceases to be mobilized, it is transformed, as Boisgillebert says, "from movable into immovable," from coin into money.

214. From the very earliest development of the circulation of commodities, there is also developed the necessity and the passionate desire to hold fast the product of the first metamorphosis. This product is the transformed shape of the commodity, or its gold-chrysalis.

Commodities are thus sold, not for the purpose of buying others, but in order to replace their commodity-form by their money-form.

From being the mere means of affecting the circulation of commodities, the change of form becomes the end and aim.

The changed form of the commodity is thus prevented from functioning as its unconditionally alienable form, or as its merely transient money-form.

The money becomes petrified into a hoard, and the seller becomes a hoarder of money.

215. In the early stages of the circulation of commodities, it is the surplus use-values alone that are converted into money.

Gold and silver thus become of themselves social expressions of a superfluity of wealth.

This naive form of hoarding becomes perpetuated in those communities in which the traditional mode of production is carried on for the supply of a fixed and limited circle of home wants.

It is thus with the people of Asia, and particularly of the East Indies.

Vanderlint, who fancied that the prices in a country are determined by the amount of gold and silver found in it, asks himself why Indian commodities are so cheap?

From 1602 to 1734, he remarks, they buried 150 million pounds sterling of silver, which originally came from America to Europe. In ten years from 1856 to 1866, England exported to India and China £120,000,000 in silver, which had been received in exchange for Australian gold.

Most of the silver exported to China makes its way to India.

216. As the production of commodities further develops, every producer of commodities is compelled to make sure of the *nexus rerum*, or the social pledge.

His wants are constantly making themselves felt, and necessitate the purchase of other people's commodities, while the production and sale of his own goods require time and depend upon circumstances.

In order to be able to buy without selling, he must have sold previously without buying.

This operation conducted upon a general scale, appears to imply a contradiction.

But the precious metals, at the source of their production, are directly exchanged for other commodities.

And here we have sales (by the owners of commodities) without purchasers (by the owners of gold and silver).

And subsequent sales by other producers unfollowed by purchases, merely bringing about the distribution of newly produced precious metals among all the owners of commodities.

In this way and all along the line of exchange, hoards of gold and silver of varied extent are accumulated.

With the possibility of hoarding and storing up exchange value in the shape of a particular commodity arises also the greed for gold.

Along with the extension of circulation increases the power of money, that absolute form of social wealth ever ready for use.

"Gold is a wonderful thing! Whoever possesses it is lord of all he wants. By means of gold one can even get souls out of paradise." (Columbus in his letter from Jamaica, 1503).

Since gold does not disclose what has been transformed into it, everything, commodity or not, is convertible into gold.

Everything becomes saleable and buyable. The circulation becomes the great social retort into which everything is thrown, to come out again a gold crystal.

Not even are the bones of the saints, and still less are the more delicate, besides most sacred, things—sensual human intercourse—able to withstand this alchemy.

NOTE—Henry III., most Christian king of France, robbed cloisters of their relics and turned them into money. It is well known what part of the despoiling of the Delphic Temple, by the Phocians, played in the history of Greece.

Temples with the ancients served as the dwellings of the gods of commodities, they were "sacred banks." With the Phoenicians, a trading people par excellence, money was the transmuted shape of everything.

It was, therefore, quite in order that the virgins, who at the feast of the Goddess of Love, gave themselves up to strangers, should offer to the Goddess the piece of money they received.

"Gold, yellow, glittering, precious gold,
Thus much of this will make black, white; foul, fair;
Wrong, right; base, noble; old, young; coward, valiant;
.... What this, you gods? Why, this
Will lug your priests and servants from your side;
Pluck stout men's pillows from below their heads;
This yellow slave
Will knit and break religions; bless the accurs'd;
Make the hoar leprosy ador'd, place thieves,
And give them title, knee and approbation,
With Senators on the bench; this is it
That makes the wappon'd widow wed again;
.... Come damned earth,
Thou common whore of mankind."
(Shakespere: Timon of Athens).

Just as every qualitative difference between commodities is extinguished in money, so money on its side, like the radical lever that it is, does away with all distinctions.

But money itself is a commodity, an external object, capable of becoming the private property of individuals. Thus social power becomes the private power of private persons.

The ancients, therefore, denounced money as subversive of the economical and moral order of things.

Modern society, which, soon after its birth, pulled Plutus by the hair of the head from the bowels of the earth, greets gold as its Holy Grail—as the glittering incarnation of the very principle of its own life.

217. A commodity in its capacity as a use-value, satisfies a particular want, and is a particular element of material wealth.

But the value of a commodity measures the degree of attraction for all other elements of material wealth, and, therefore, measures the social wealth of its owner.

To a barbarian owner of commodities, and even to a West European peasant, value is the same as value-form, and therefore to him an increase in his hoard of gold and silver is an increase in value.

It is true that the value of money varies, at one time in consequence of a variation in its own value, at another in consequence of a variation in the value of commodities.

But this, on the one hand, does not prevent 200 ounces of gold from still containing more value than 100 ounces; nor, on the other hand, does it hinder the actual metallic form of this article from continuing to be the universal equivalent-form for all other commodities, and the immediate incarnation of all human labor.

The desire after hoarding is, in its very nature, insatiable.

In its qualitative aspect, or formally considered, money has no bounds to its efficacy; that is, it is the universal representative of material wealth, because it is directly convertible into any other commodity.

But, at the same time, every actual sum of money is limited in amount, and, therefore, as a means of purchasing has a limited efficacy.

This antagonism between the quantitative limits of money and its qualitative boundlessness, continually acts as a spur to the hoarder in his Sisyphus-like labor of accumulating.

It is with him like it is with the conqueror who sees in every new country annexed only a new boundary.

218. In order that gold may be held as money, and made to form a hoard, it must be prevented from circulating, or from transforming itself into a means of enjoyment.

A hoarder, therefore, makes a sacrifice of the lusts of the flesh to his gold-fetish.

He acts in earnest up to the gospel of abstention.

On the other hand, he can withdraw from circulation no more than what he has thrown into it in the shape of commodities.

The more he produces the more he is able to sell.

Hard work, saving, and avarice are, therefore, his three cardinal virtues, and to sell much and buy little the sum of his political economy.

219. By the side of the gross form of a hoard, we find also its aesthetic form in the possession of gold and silver articles.

This grows with the wealth of civil society.

In this way there is created, on the one hand, a constantly extended market for gold and silver, unconnected with their functions as money, and, on the other hand, a latent source of supply, to which recourse is had principally in times of crises and social disturbances.

220. Hoarding serves various purposes in the economy of the metallic currency.

Its first function arises out of the conditions to which the currency of gold and silver coins is subject.

We have seen how, along with the continual fluctuations in the extent and rapidity of the circulation of commodities and in their prices, the quantity of money current unceasingly ebbs and flows.

This mass must, therefore, be capable of expansion and contraction.

At one time money must be attracted to act as circulating coin; at another, circulating coin must be repelled in order to act again as more or less stagnant money.

In order that the mass of money actually current may constantly saturate the absorbing power of the circulation, it is necessary that the quantity of gold and silver, in a country, be greater than the quantity required to function as coin.

This condition is filled by money taking the form of hoards.

These reserves serve as conduits for the supply or withdrawal of money to or from the circulation, which in this way never overflows its banks.

b. *Means of payment.*

221. In the simple form of the circulation of commodities, hitherto considered, we found a given value always presented to us in a double shape—as a commodity at one pole, as money at the opposite pole.

The owners of commodities came, therefore, in contact as the respective representatives of what were already equivalents.

But with the development of circulation, conditions arise under which the alienation of commodities becomes separated, by an interval of time, from the realization of their prices.

It will be sufficient to indicate the most simple of these conditions.

One sort of article requires a longer, another a shorter, time for its production.

Again, the production of different commodities depends on different seasons of the year.

One sort of commodity may be born on its own market place, another has to make a long journey to market.

Commodity owner No. 1 may, therefore, be ready to sell before No. 2 is ready to buy.

When the same transactions are continually repeated between the same persons, the conditions of sale are regulated in accordance with the conditions of production.

On the other hand, the use of a given commodity—of a house, for instance—is sold (in common parlance, let) for a definite period.

Here, it is only at the end of the term that the buyer has actually received the use-value of the commodity.

He, therefore, buys it before he pays for it.

The vendor sells an existing commodity, the purchaser buys as the mere representative of money; the vendor becomes a creditor, the purchaser becomes a debtor.

Since the metamorphosis of commodities, or the development of their value-form, appears here under a new aspect, money also acquires a fresh function; it becomes the means of payment.

222. The character of creditor, or debtor, results here from the simple circulation.

The change in the form of that circulation stamps buyer and seller with this new die.

At first, therefore, these new parts are just as transient and alternating as those of seller and buyer, and are in turns played by the same actors.

But the opposition is not nearly so pleasant, and is far more capable of crystalization.

The same character can, however, be assumed independently of the circulation of commodities.

The class struggle of the ancient world took the form chiefly of a contest between debtors and creditors, which in Rome ended in the ruin of the plebeian debtors.

They were displaced by slaves.

In the Middle Ages the contest ended with the ruin of one feudal debtors, who lost their political power, together with the economical basis on which it was established.

Nevertheless, the money relation of debtor and creditor that existed at these two periods reflected only the deeper-lying antagonism between the general economical conditions of existence of the classes in question.

223. Let us return to the circulation of commodities.

The appearance of the two equivalents, commodities and money, at the two poles of the process of sale has ceased to be simultaneous.

The money functions now:

First, as a measure of value in the determination of the prices of the commodities sold; the price fixed by the contract measures the obligation of the debtor, or the sum of money he has to pay at a fixed date.

Secondly, it serves as an ideal means of purchase.

Although existing in the promise of the buyer to pay, it causes the commodity to change hands.

It is not before the day fixed for payment that the means of payment actually steps into circulation; leaves the hands of the buyer for that of the seller.

The circulating medium was transformed into a hoard because the process stopped short after the first phase; because the converted shape of the commodity, namely, the money, was withdrawn from circulation.

The means of payment enters the circulation, but only after the commodity has left it.

The money is no longer the means that brings about the process.

It only brings it to a close by stepping in as the absolute form of the existence of exchange-value, or as the universal commodity.

The seller turned his commodity into money in order thereby to satisfy some want; the hoarder did the same in order to keep his commodity in its money-shape, and the debtor in order to be able to pay; if he does not pay, his goods will be sold by the sheriff.

The value-form of commodities is, therefore, now the end and aim of sale, and that owing to a social necessity springing out of the process of circulation itself.

224. The buyer converts money back into commodities before he has turned commodities into money; in other words, he achieves the second metamorphosis of commodities before the first.

The sellers' commodity circulates, and realizes its price, but only in the shape of a legal claim on money.

It is converted into use-value before it has been converted into money.

The completion of its first metamorphosis is followed only at a latter period.

225. The obligations falling due within a given period represents the sum of the prices of the commodities, the sale of which gave rise to those obligations.

The quantity of gold necessary to realize this sum depends, in the first instance, on the rapidity of currency of the means of payment.

The quantity is conditioned by two circumstances:

First, the relation between debtors and creditors forms a sort of chain, in such a way that A, when he receives money from his debtor B, straightway hands it over to C, his creditor, and so on.

The second circumstance is the length of the interval between the different due days of the obligations.

The continuous chain of payments or retarded first metamorphosis, is essentially different from the interlacing of the series of metamorphosis which we considered on a former page.

By the currency of the circulating medium the connection between the buyers and sellers is not merely expressed.

This connection is originated by, and exist in, the circulation alone.

Contrarywise, the movement of the means of payment expresses a social relation that was in existence long before.

226. The fact that a number of sales takes place simultaneously, and side by side, limits the extent to which coin can be replaced by the rapidity of currency.

On the other hand, this fact is a new lever in economizing the means of payment.

In proportion as payments are concentrated at one spot, special institutions and methods are developed for their liquidation.

Such, in the Middle Ages, were the *virements* at Lyons.

The debts of A from B, to B from C, to C from A, and so on, had only to be confronted by each other in order to annul each other, to a certain extent like positive and negative quantities.

There thus remained only a single balance to pay.

The greater the amount of payments concentrated, the less is the balance relative to the amount, and the less is the mass of the means of payment in circulation.

227. The function of money as the means of payment implies a contradiction without a "*terminus medius.*"

In so far as the payments balance one another, money functions ideally as money of account; as a measure of value.

In so far as actual payments have to be made, money does not serve as a circulating medium, as a mere transient agent in the interchange of products, but as the individual incarnation of social labor, as the universal commodity.

This contradiction comes to a head in those phases of individual and commercial crises which are known as money crises.

Such a crisis occurs only when the ever-lengthening chain of payments, and an artificial system of settling them, has been fully developed.

Whenever there is a general and extensive disturbance of this mechanism, no matter what its cause, money becomes immediately transformed, from its merely ideal shape of money of account, into hard cash.

Profane commodities can no longer replace it.

The use-value of commodities become useless, and their value vanishes in the presence of its independent form.

On the eve of a crisis the bourgeois, with the self-sufficiency that springs from intoxicated prosperity, declares money to be a vain imagination.

Commodities alone are money.

But now the cry is everywhere: Money alone is a commodity.

As the hare pants after fresh water, so pants his soul after money, the only wealth.

In a crisis, the antithesis between commodities and their value form, money, becomes heightened into an absolute contradiction.

Hence, in such events, the form under which money appears is of no importance.

The money famine continues, whether payments have to be made in gold or credit money, such as bank notes.

228. If we now consider the sum total of money current during a given period, we shall find that, given the rapidity of the currency of the circulating medium and of the means of payment, it is equal to the sum of the prices to be realized, plus the sum of the payments falling due, minus the payments that balance each other; minus, finally, the number of circuits in which the same piece of coin serves in turn as means of circulation and as means of payment.

Hence, even when prices, rapidity of currency, and the extent of economy in payments is given, the quantity of money current and the mass of commodities circulating during a given period, such as a day, no longer correspond.

Money that represents commodities long withdrawn from circulation, continues to be current.

Commodities circulate whose equivalent will not appear on the scene till some future day.

Moreover the debts contracted each day, and the payments falling due on the same day, are quite incommensurable.

229. Credit money springs directly out of the function of money as means of payment.

Certificates of the debts owing for purchased commodities circulate for the purpose of transferring those debts to others.

On the other hand, to the same extent the system of credit is extended, so is the function of money as the means of payment.

In that character it takes various forms peculiar to itself, under which it makes itself at home in the sphere of great commercial transactions.

Gold and silver coin, on the other hand, are mostly relegated to the sphere of retail trade.

230. When the production of commodities has sufficiently extended itself money begins to serve as the means of payment beyond the sphere of the circulation of commodities.

It becomes the commodity that is the subject matter of all contracts.

Rent, taxes, and such like payments are transformed from payments in kind into money payments.

To what extent this transformation depends upon the condition of production is shown, to take one example, by the fact that the Roman empire twice failed to levy all contributions in money.

The unspeakable misery of the French agricultural population under Louis XIV — a misery so elegantly denounced by Boisgillebert, Marshal Vaban, and others — was due not only to the weight of taxes, but also to the conversion of taxes in kind to money taxes.

In Asia, on the other hand, the fact that the state taxes are chiefly composed of rents payable in kind depends upon conditions of production that are reproduced with the regularity of a natural phenomena.

And this mode of payment tends, in turn, to maintain the ancient mode of production.

It is one of the secrets of the conservation of the Ottoman Empire.

If the foreign trade forced upon Japan by Europeans should lead to the substitution of money rents for rents in kind, it will be all up with the exemplary agriculture of that country.

The narrow economical conditions under which that agriculture is carried on will be swept away.

231. In every country certain days become, by habit, recognized settling days for various large and recurrent payments.

These dates depend, apart from other revolutions in the wheel of reproduction, on conditions closely connected with the seasons.

They also regulate the dates of payments that have no direct connection with the circulation of commodities, such as taxes, rents, and so on.

The quantity of money requisite to make the payments, falling due on those dates all over the country, causes periodical, though merely superficial perturbations in the economy in the medium of payment.

232. From the law of the rapidity of currency of the means of payment, it follows that the quantity of the means of payment required for all periodical payments, whatever their source, is in the inverse proportion to the length of their periods.

233. The development of money into a medium of payment, makes it necessary to accumulate money against the date fixed for the payment of sums oweing.

While hoarding, as a distinct mode of acquiring riches, vanishes with the progress of civil society, the formation of reserves of the means of payment grows with the progress.

c. Universal money.

234. When money leaves the home sphere of circulation, it strips off the local garb which it there assumes as the standard of price, of coin, or tokens, and of a symbol of value, and returns to its original form of bullion.

In the trade between the markets of the world the value of commodities is expressed so as to be universally recognized.

Hence their independent value-form also, in these cases, confronts them under the shape of universal money.

It is only in the markets of the world that money acquires, to the full extent the character of the commodity whose bodily form is also the immediate social incarnation of human labor in the abstract.

Its real mode of existence in this sphere adequately corresponds to its ideal concept.

235. Within the sphere of home circulation there can be but one commodity which, by serving as a measure of value, becomes money.

In the markets of the world a double measure holds sway—gold and silver.

236. Money of the world serves as a universal means of payment, as the universal means of purchasing, as the universally recognized embodiment of wealth.

Its function as a means of payment in the settling of international balances is its chief one.

Hence the watchward of the mercantilists—Balance of Trade.

Gold and silver serve as international means of purchasing chiefly and necessarily in those periods when the customary equilibrium in the interchange of products between different nations is suddenly disturbed.

And, lastly, it serves, as the universally recognized embodiment of social wealth, whenever the question is not of buying or paying, but of transferring wealth from one country to another, and whenever this transference in the form of commodities is rendered impossible, either by special conjunctures in the markets, or by the purpose itself that is intended.

237. Just as every country needs a reserve of money for its home circulation, so, too, it requires one for the external circulation in the markets of the world.

The function of hoards, therefore, rise in part out of the function of money as the medium of home circulation and home payments, and in part out of the function of money of the world.

For this latter function, the genuine money commodity, actual gold and silver, is necessary.

On that account, Sir James Stuart, in order to distinguish them from their purely local substitutes, calls gold and silver, "Money of the World."

238. The current of the stream of gold and silver is a double one.

On the one hand, it spreads itself from its sources over all the markets of the world in order to become absorbed, to various extents, into the different national spheres of circulation, to fill the conduits of currency, to replace abraided gold and silver coins, to supply the material of articles of luxury, and to petrify into hoards.

The first current is started by the countries that exchange their labor, realized in commodities, for the labor embodied in the precious metals by gold and silver producing countries.

On the other hand, there is a continual flowing backwards and forwards of gold and silver between the different national spheres of circulation—a current whose motion depends on the ceaseless fluctuations in the course of exchange.

239. Countries in which the bourgeois form of production is developed, to a certain extent, limit the hoards concentrated in the

strong rooms of the banks to the minimum required for the proper performance of their peculiar functions.

Whenever these hoards are strikingly above their average level, it is, with some exceptions, an indication of stagnation in the circulation of commodities, or an interruption in the even flow of their metamorphoses.

Part II. The Transformation of Money Into Capital

Chapter IV. The General Formula Of Capital

What is the starting point of capital? The circulation of commodities.

The production of commodities, their circulation, and that more developed form of their circulation called commerce, these form the historical ground work from which it arises.

The modern history of capital dates from the creation, in the sixteenth century, of a world embracing commerce and a world embracing market.

If we abstract from the material substance—the different use-values—exchanged and consider only the economic forms produced by the circulation of commodities, what is the final result? Money.

This is the first form in which capital appears.

As a matter of history, capital, as opposed to landed property; invariably takes the form, at first, of money; it appears as moneyed wealth, as the capital of the merchant and usurer.

How does all new capital come on the market? Whether of commodities, labor, or money, it comes on the market in the shape of money that by a definite process has to be transformed into capital.

What distinction do we first see, between money, that is money only, and, money that is, capital? Merely the difference in their form of circulation.

What is the simplest form of the circulation of commodities? C—M—C, selling in order to buy.

What is the specifically different form, of the circulation of the capital? M—C—M, buying in order to sell.

Money that circulates in the circuit M—C—M, is thereby transformed into, is potentially, capital.

What have these two forms in common? Both circuits are resolvable into the same two antithetical phases, C—M, a sale, and M—C, a purchase.

In each of these phases the same material elements—a commodity and money, and the same dramatical characters—a buyer and seller, confront one another.

Each circuit is the unity of the same two antithetical phases.

And, in each case this unity is brought about by the intervention of three contracting parties, of whom one only sells, another only buys, while the third both buys and sells.

What are most distinguished features between C—M—C and M—C—M? The inverted order of succession of the two phases.

The circulation of commodities begins and ends with a commodity; the movement is brought about by the intervention of money.

What is the purpose aimed at? The exchange of labor embodied in one commodity, which is not a use-value to its owner, for the same amount of labor embodied in another commodity, which is a use-value to him.

For example, a farmer exchanges corn for money, and with the money purchases clothes.

If we leave out the intermediary—money—we have corn exchanged for clothes, a commodity exchanged for a commodity of equal value but of different quality; C—M—C ends with a commodity, which falls out of circulation into consumption, the satisfaction of wants, it thus fulfills the purpose aimed at.

How does the inverted order of succession differ from M—C—M? The circuit M—C—M begins and ends with money.

What is its purpose and aim? The exchange of money for more money, for if we leave out the intermediary—commodity—it is an exchange of money for money.

In this circuit, M—C—M, money is transformed from money, as mere money, into capital.

If a merchant buys one ton of cotton for $100, and resells it for $110, he has, in fact, exchanged $100 for $110—money for more money.

The exact form of this process is, therefore, M—C—M, where M=M plus M', the original sum plus an increment.

This excess over the original value is what I call "surplus value."

The value originally advanced, not only remains intact while in circulation, but adds to itself surplus-value.

It is this movement that converts it into capital.

If now the $110 be spent as money, what is the result? They no longer play their part, and are no longer capital.

If withdrawn from circulation they petrify into a hoard, and though they remain in that state till doomsday, not a single cent would accrue to them.

If the expansion of value is aimed at there is just as much inducement to augment the $110 as that of the $100.

The circulation of commodities is a means of carrying out a purpose unconnected with circulation, namely, the appropriation of use-values—the satisfaction of wants.

The circulation of money, as capital, is an end in itself, for the expansion takes place only within the constantly renewed movements.

Thus the conscious representative of this movement, the possessor of money, becomes a capitalist.

What is the real aim of a capitalist? The restless never-ending process of profit making alone.

And it is only in so far as the appropriation of ever more and more wealth, in the abstract, becomes the sole motive of his operations that he functions as a capitalist.

If we take in turn each of the two different forms which self-expanding value assumes in the course of its life, we arrive at these two propositions: Capital is money; capital is commodities.

Value is the active factor in the process, it continually changes its form; at one time it is money, at another it is commodities.

At the same time it changes its form it changes its magnitude, differentiates itself by throwing off surplus-value from itself; the original value expands spontaneously.

Money itself is only one of the two forms of value, and unless it takes the form of some commodity it does not become capital.

Buying in order to sell, or, speaking more accurately, buying to sell dearer, M—C—M, appears certainly to be a form peculiar to one kind of capital alone; namely, merchants' capital.

But industrial capital, too, is money that is changed into commodities, and by the sale of these commodities is reconverted into money.

The events that take place outside the sphere of circulation, in the interval between buying and selling, do not affect the form of this movement.

Lastly, in the case of interest-bearing capital the circulation is abridged.

We have the result without the intermediary stage, in the form of M—M; money that is worth more money, value that is greater than itself.

M—C—M is, in reality, the general formula of capital as it appears prima facie within the sphere of circulation.

Chapter V.   Contradictions In The General Formula Of Capital

The form which circulation takes when money becomes capital is opposed to all the laws we have hitherto investigated bearing on the nature of commodities, value, money, and even of circulation itself.

What distinguishes this form from the simple circulation of commodities is the inverted order of succession of the two antithetical processes, sale and purchase.

How can this purely formal distinction between these processes change their character, as it were by magic? The inverted order of succession does not take us outside the sphere of circulation of commodities.

What, then, must we first find out? If there is in the simple circulation of commodities anything permitting an expansion of value that enters into circulation.

Let us take the process of circulation in a form under which it presents itself as a simple and direct exchange of commodities. This is always the case where two owners of commodities buy from each other, and on the settling day, the amounts mutually oweing are equal and balance each other.

The money in this case is money of account, and serves to express the value of the commodities by their price, but it is not itself in the shape of hard cash confronted by them.

How can there be any gain in the exchange of equivalents? Both part with goods that, as use-values, are of no service to them, and receive others that they can make use of.

Again, A who sells wine and buys corn from B, possibly produces more wine with given labor-time than B could, and B, on the other hand, more corn than wine-grower A could.

A, therefore, may get, for the same exchange value, more corn and B more wine, than each would respectively get by producing their own corn and wine.

With reference to use-value there is good ground for saying that exchange is a transaction in which both sides gain.

But this has reference to use-value only.

Can there be any increase of value by simple circulation? In the simple circulation of commodities there is nothing but the mere change of form of the commodities; the same exchange value remains throughout in the hands of the owner of the commodity, first in the shape of his own commodity, then in the form of money for which he exchanged it, and, lastly, in the shape of the commodity he buys with the money.

If commodities, or commodities and money of equal value are exchanged, it is plain that no one can extract more from circulation than he throws into it.

What then is the incentive to the act of exchange of commodities? The material varieties of these commodities makes buyers and sellers mutually dependent, because none of them possess the objects of his own wants, and each holds in his hand the object of another's wants.

As we can find no increase of value in the exchange of equivalents, how must we now deal with circulation? Assume the exchange of non-equivalents.

Suppose, then, by some inexplicable privilege, the seller is enabled to sell his commodities above their value, what is worth $100 for $110, in which the price is nominally raised 10 per cent.

After he has sold he becomes a buyer, and meets a third commodity owner who is a seller, and also enjoys the privilege of selling 10 per cent too dear.

The net result is, that all commodity owners sell their goods to one another 10 per cent above their value, which amounts to the same thing as to sell them at their true value.

If we make the opposite assumption, that the buyer has the privilege of buying 10 per cent below the value of the goods he buys, he lost 10 per cent as seller before he bought, the result is just the same.

The creation of surplus-value, that which turns money into capital, can be explained neither on the assumption that commodities are sold above their value, nor that they are bought below their value.

Let us try again, perhaps our difficulty may have arisen from treating the actors as personifications instead of individuals.

A may be clever enough to get the advantage of B or C without their being able to retaliate.

A sells wine, worth $40 to B, and gets from him corn to the value of $50. A has converted his $40 into $50, has made more money out of less, has turned his commodities into capital.

Before the exchange we had $40 worth of wine in the hands of A and $50 worth of corn in the hands of B, a total value of $90.

After the exchange we have the same total value of $90.

The value has not increased one iota; it is only distributed differently between A and B; the result would be the same if A had directly stolen $10 from B.

The sum of values in circulation can clearly not be augmented by a change in their distribution.

The capitalist class, as a whole, in any country, cannot overreach themselves. Turn and twist them as we may the fact remains unaltered.

If equivalents are exchanged, no surplus-value results, and if non-equivalents are exchanged, still no surplus-value; circulation, or the exchange of commodities, begets no value.

The reason is now plain why, in analyzing the standard form of capital — the form under which capital determines the economic organization of modern society — we left out of consideration its most popular and antedeluvian forms, merchant's capital and moneylender's capital.

The circuit M — C — M, buying in order to sell dearer, is seen most clearly in genuine merchants' capital

Since the movement takes place entirely within the sphere of circulation, and, that there can be no formation of surplus-values in circulation alone.

It can only have its origin in the twofold advantage gained, over both the selling and buying producers, by the merchant who parasitically shoves himself in between them.

This applies still more to moneylender's capital.

It is reduced to the two extremes without a mean, M—M: money exchanged for more money.

A form that is incompatible with the nature of money, and therefore remains inexplicable from the standpoint of the circulation of commodities,

Aristotle says: "Since schrematistic is a double science, one part belonging to commerce, the other to economics, the latter being necessary and praiseworthy, the former based upon circulation and with justice disapproved (for it is not based on nature, but on mutual cheating), therefore the usurer is most rightly hated, because money itself is the source of his gain, and is not used for the purpose for which it was invented."

For it originated for the exchange of commodities, but interest makes out of money more money.

The begotten are like those who beget them.

But interest is money of money, so that of all modes of making a living this is the most contrary to nature.

Merchant's capital and interest bearing capital are derivative forms, and appear in the course of history before the modern standard form of capital.

We have shown that surplus-value cannot be created by circulation, and, therefore, that in its formation something must take place in the background which is not apparent in the circulation itself.

But can surplus-value possibly originate anywhere else than in circulation, which is the sum total of all the mutual relations of commodity-owners so far as they are determined by their commodities?

Apart from circulation, the commodity-owner is in relation only with his own commodity. So far as regards value, that relation is limited to this: That the commodity contains a quantity of his own labor, that quantity being measured by a definite social standard.

This quantity is expressed by the value of the commodity, and since the value is reckoned in money of account, this quantity is also expressed by the price, which we will suppose to be $10.

But his labor is not represented both by the value of the commodity and by a surplus over that value, not by a price of 10 that is also a price of 11; not by a value that is greater than itself.

The commodity-owner can, by his labor, create value, but not self-expanding value.

He can increase the value of his commodity by adding fresh labor, and, therefore, more value to the value in hand, by making, for instance, leather into boots.

The same material has now more value, because it contains a greater quantity of labor.

The boots have, therefore, more value than the leather, but the value of the leather remains what it was; it has not expanded itself — has not, during the making of the boots, annexed surplus-value.

It is therefore impossible that, outside the sphere of circulation, a producer can, without coming into contact with other commodity — owners, expand value, and consequently convert money or commodities into capital.

It is impossible for capital to be produced by circulation, and it is equally impossible for it to originate apart from circulation.

It must have its origin both in circulation and yet not in circulation. We have got a double result.

The conversion of money into capital has to be explained on the basis of the laws that regulate the exchange of commodities, in such a way that the starting point is the exchange of equivalents.

Our friend Moneybags, who as yet is only an embryo capitalist, must buy his commodities at their value, must sell them at their value, and yet at the end of the process must withdraw more value from circulation than he threw into it.

His development into a full-grown capitalist must take place, both within the sphere of circulation and without it.

These are the conditions of the problem.

Hic Rhodus, Hic Salta! (here is the rose, now dance).

Chapter VI. The Buying And Selling Of Labor-Power

We have seen that there can be no surplus-value created by the act of exchange, nor can any change of value take place in the money, either as a medium of exchange nor as a means of payment, as hard cash it is value petrified, never varying.

Then where must the change take place? In the commodity bought, but not in its value, for it is paid for at its full value, equivalents are exchanged.

We are, therefore, forced to the conclusion that the change originates in the consumption of the commodity. To extract value from the consumption, our friend Moneybags must find, within the sphere of circulation, in the market, a commodity possessing the peculiar property of being itself an embodiment of labor and also whose actual consumption is the creating of value.

The possessor of money does find such a special commodity in labor-power.

What is labor-power? Those mental and physical capabilities existing in a human being, which he uses whenever he produces a use-value of any description.

The owner of money can find labor-power offered for sale as a commodity, only under certain conditions.

What are these conditions? First, there must be free laborers—free in the double sense, free to dispose of his labor-power, as his own commodity, and free from all the means of production, whereby he could realize the fruit of his labor-power.

Second, he must look upon his labor as his own property, his own commodity.

To do this he can sell it only for a definite period, for were he to sell it once for all, he would renounce his ownership over it, sell himself, and become himself a commodity—a slave.

Let us examine more closely this peculiar commodity, labor-power.

Like all others, it has value.

How is this value determined? By the labor-time necessary for its production, and consequently also for the reproduction of this special article.

So far as it has value, it represents no more than a definite quantity of the average labor of society incorporated in it.

The labor-time requisite for the production of labor-power reduces itself to that necessary for the production of the means of subsistence.

Labor-power becomes a reality only by its exercise, it sets itself in action only by working.

Thereby a definite quantity of brains, muscles and nerves, etc., is wasted, and these require to be restored.

If the owner of labor-power works today, tomorrow he must again be able to repeat the process in the same condition as regards health and strength.

His means of subsistence must, therefore, be sufficient to maintain him in his normal state as a laboring individual.

The owner of labor power is mortal, and the conversion of money into capital assumes that the laborer must perpetuate himself.

The labor-power withdrawn from the market by wear and tear and death must be replaced by, at least, an equal amount of fresh labor-power.

Hence the sum of the means of subsistence must include the means of subsistence necessary for the maintenance of the family.

The value of labor-power resolves itself into the value of a definite quantity of the means of subsistence.

It therefore varies with the value of the means, or with the quantity of labor requisite for their production.

Some of the means of subsistence, such as food and fuel, are consumed daily, and a fresh supply must be provided daily.

Others, such as clothes and furniture, last for longer periods, and are replaced only at longer periods.

One article must be bought, and paid for, daily, another weekly, another quarterly, and so on.

If the total of the commodities required daily for the production of labor-power=A, and those required weekly=B, and those required quarterly=C the daily average of these commodities=365 A plus 52 B plus 4 C divided by 365.

Suppose that in the amount of commodities requisite for the average day there is incorporated two hours of social labor, then two hours social labor forms the value of a day's labor-power.

If two hours social labor is incorporated in $2, then $2 is the price corresponding to the value of a day's labor-power.

Our friend Moneybags, who is intent on turning his $2 into capital, pays this value.

The minimum limit of the value of labor-power is determined by the value of the means of subsistence physically indispensable.

If the price of labor-power fall to this minimum it falls below its value, for under such circumstances it can be maintained and developed only in a crippled state.

But the value of every commodity is determined by the labor-time requisite to turn it out in a normal state.

The labor-power is sold, although it is not paid for until a later date.

It will be useful for a clear understanding of the relation between the parties, to assume that the possessor of labor-power, on the occasion of each sale, immediately receives the price to be paid for it.

We know now how the value paid by the purchaser of this peculiar commodity, labor-power, is determined.

The consumption of labor-power is at one and the same time the production of commodities, and of surplus-value.

The money owner buys everything necessary for this purpose.

The consumption of labor-power, like the consumption of any other commodity, takes place outside the sphere of circulation.

Accompanied by both Mr. Moneybags and the possessor of labor-power, we take leave, for a time, of this noisy sphere, and follow them both into the hidden abode of production, on whose threshold there stares us in the face: "No admittance except on business."

Here we will see, not only how capital produces, but how capital is produced.

We shall at last force the secret of profit making.

The sphere we are deserting, in which the sale and purchase of labor-power goes on, is a very Eden of the innate rights of man.

There alone rule Freedom, Equality, Property, and Bentham.

Freedom, because both buyer and seller of a commodity—labor-power—are constrained only by their own free will.

They contract as free agents, and the agreement they come to is but the form in which they give legal expression to their common will.

Equality, because each enter into relation with the other as with a simple owner of commodities, and they exchange equivalent for equivalent.

Property, because each disposes only of what is his own.

And Bentham, because each looks only to himself.

The only force that brings them together and puts them in relation with each other, is the selfishness, the gain, and the private interest of each.

Each looks to himself only, and no one troubles himself about the rest, and just because they do so, do they all, in accordance with the pre-established harmony of things, or under the auspices of an all-shrewd providence, work together for their mutual advantage, for the common weal and in the interest of all.

On leaving the sphere of simple circulation, or of exchange of commodities, which furnishes the "Free-Trader Vulgaris" with his views and ideas, and with the standard by which he judges a society based on capital and wages, we think we can perceive a change in physiognomy of our dramatic characters.

He who before was the money-owner now strides in front as capitalist; the possessor of labor-power follows as his laborer.

The one with an air of importance, smirking, intent on business; the other, timid and holding back, like one who is bringing his own hide to market and has nothing to expect but—a hiding.

Part III. The Production of Absolute Surplus Value

Chapter VII. The Labor-Process And The Process Of Producing Surplus-Value.

Section I. The labor-process, or the production of use-value

The capitalist buys labor-power in order to use it. He consumes it by setting the seller of it to work. By working the latter becomes actually, what before he only was potentially, labor-power in action, a laborer.

In order that his labor may reappear in a commodity he must expend it on some useful thing, on something capable of satisfying a want of some sort.

Hence the capitalist sets him to work at producing a use-value, a specific article.

Labor is a process in which both man and nature participate, and in which man of his own accord starts, regulates, and controls the material reaction between himself and nature.

He opposes himself to nature as one of her own forces, setting in motion arms, legs, head and hands, the natural forces of his body, in order to appropriate nature's productions in a form adapted to his own wants.

Besides the exertions of the bodily organs, the process demands that, during the whole operation, the workman's will be steadily in consonance with his purpose.

This means close attention.

The less he is attracted by the nature of the work, and the less he enjoys it as something that gives play to his mental and bodily powers, the closer his attention is forced to be.

The elementary factors of the process are:

First. The personal activity of man — work itself;

Second. The subject of that work;

Third. Its instruments.

The soil (economically speaking this includes water) in the virgin state in which it supplies man with necessaries or the means of subsistence ready to hand, exists independently of him, and is the universal subject of human labor.

All those things which labor merely separates from immediate connection with their environment are subjects of labor spontaneously provided by nature.

Such are fish, which we catch and take from their element, the water; timber, which we fell in the virgin forest; and ores, which we extract from their veins.

If the subject of labor has passed through labor we call it raw material; such is ore already extracted and ready for smelting.

All raw material is the subject of labor, but every subject of labor is not raw material; it can only become so by having undergone some alteration by means of labor.

Instruments of labor.

An instrument of labor is a thing, or complex of things (machine), which the laborer interposes between himself and the subject of his labor, and which serves as the conductor of his activity.

The first thing of which the laborer possesses himself is not the subject of labor, but the instrument.

Among the instruments of labor, those of a mechanical nature, which, taken as a whole, we may call the bones and muscles of production, those such as pipes, tubs, jars, baskets, etc., which serve only to hold the materials for labor we may call the vascular system of production.

In a wider sense we may include among the instruments of labor, all such objects as are necessary for carrying on the labor process.

We find the earth to be a universal instrument of this sort, for it furnishes a standing place for the laborer, and a field of employment for his activities.

Among instruments that are the result of previous labor, and also belong to this class, we find workshops, canals, railroads, etc.

In the labor process, therefore, man's activity, with the help of the instruments of labor, effects an alteration in the material worked upon.

The process disappears in the product; the latter is a use-value, nature's material adapted by a change of form to the wants of man.

Labor has incorporated itself with its subject; the former is materialized, the latter transformed.

That which in the laborer appeared as movement now appears in the product as a fixed quality without motion.

The blacksmith forges, and the product is a forging.

If we examine the whole process from the point of view of its result, the product, it is plain that both the instruments and subject of labor are means of production, and that labor itself is productive labor.

Raw material may either form the principle substance of a product, or may enter into its formation only as an accessory.

An accessory may be consumed by the instrument of labor, as coal under a boiler, oil by a wheel, hay by a draft horse, or it may help to carry on the work itself, as materials used for heating and lighting workshops.

One and the same product may serve as raw material in very different processes.

Every object possesses various properties and is capable of being applied to different uses, and may serve as raw material in very different processes.

For example, corn is a raw material for millers, starch manufacturers, and cattle breeders, and also in its own production, as seed; coal too, is the product of, and at the same time, also the means of production in, coal-mining.

Again, a particular product may be used in one and the same process, both as instruments of labor and as raw material.

Take, for instance, the fattening of cattle, where the animal is raw material and at the same time an instrument for the production of manure.

Hence, whether a use-value is to be regarded as raw material, as instrument of labor, or as product, is determined entirely by its function in the labor process, by the position it there occupies; as this varies so does its character.

A machine which does not serve the purpose of labor is useless.

In addition, it falls a prey to the destructive influence of natural forces. Iron rusts and wood rots.

Yarn with which we neither weave nor knit is cotton wasted.

Living labor must seize upon these things and arouse them from their death sleep, change them from mere possible use-values into real and effective ones.

Bathed in the fire of labor, appropriated as part and parcel of labor's organism, and made alive for the performance of their functions in the process, they are in truth consumed, but consumed with a purpose, as elementary constituents of new use-values, of new products, ever ready as means of subsistence for individual consumption, or as means of production for some new labor-process.

Labor uses up its material factors, its subject and its instruments; consumes them, and is, therefore, a process of consumption.

Let us now return to our would-be capitalist.

We left him just after he had purchased all the necessary factors of the labor-process; its objective factors, the means of production, as well as its subjective factor labor power.

He has selected the means of production and the kind of labor-power best adapted to his particular trade.

He then proceeds to consume the commodity, labor-power, by causing the laborer to consume the means of production by his labor.

The labor-process, turned into the process by which the capitalist consumes labor-power, exhibits two characteristic phenomena.

First, the laborer works under control of the capitalist, to whom his labor belongs; the capitalist taking good care that the work is done in a proper manner, and that there is no waste of raw material, and no more wear and tear of the implements than is necessary to do the work.

Secondly, the capitalist pays for a day's labor-power, and the use of that labor-power for a day belongs to him.

The seller in giving his labor does no more in reality than part with a use-value that he has sold.

The labor-process is a process between things that the capitalist has purchased, things that have become his property. The product of this process belongs to him just as much as does the wine which is the product of a process of fermentation completed in his cellar.

Section 2.-The Production of Surplus-Values

It must be borne in mind that we are now dealing with the production of commodities, and that, up to this point, we have only considered one aspect of the process.

Just as commodities are, at the same time, use-values and values, so the process of producing them must be a labor-process, and at the same time a process of creating value.

Let us now examine production as a creation of value.

We know that the value of each commodity is determined by the, social necessary, labor-time spent in its production.

This rule also holds good in the case of the product that accrued to our capitalist as the result of the labor-process carried on for him.

Assuming this product to be 100 pounds of yarn, our first step is to calculate the quantity of labor realized in it.

First our capitalist must purchase a spinning machine, as it is a necessary instrument in the production of yarn.

We will assume that for each 100 pounds of yarn spun that the wear and tear of the machine is equal to one hour's labor time, and this will include also the buildings—factory—and other accessories.

We will assume that six hours' labor-time is embodied in the 100 pounds of cotton.

We will assume that in one day's labor-power there is embodied two hours' labor-time.

That is, a laborer will consume in 24 hours, at the standard of living, prevalent at the time, food, clothing and shelter, to the amount that will require 2 hours' labor-time to produce them.

We treat the labor expended in the production of raw material and the means of production as labor expended in the earlier stages of spinning.

We will further assume that it requires one hour's labor-time to produce $1.00.

Hence our capitalist has paid, at their full value, for the raw material—cotton—$6.00 for the means of production—factory and machinery that enters in the product, yarn—$1, for labor power $2. Total, $9.

The value of the raw material and the factory and accessories never vary no matter what form they may take.

Now our capitalist starts his labor-power to work transforming his cotton into yarn.

And finds at the end of one hour twelve and one-half pounds of cotton has been transformed into yarn, that twelve and one-half pounds of yarn has one hour's more labor embodied in it than was embodied in the cotton, hence $1 in value has been added to the cotton, and yarn has a value of 15 cents per pound.

At the end of the next hour 25 pounds of cotton has been converted into yarn, the value of $2 has been added to 25 pounds of cotton.

Should the process stop here, our capitalist would be in a bad predicament.

The cost of raw material and means of production are equal to: Factory and cotton (7 cent per pound), 25 pounds, $1.75; labor-power, $2.00; total, $3.75.

Value of 25 pounds of yarn (15 cents per pound), $3.75.

Stock on hand, 75 pounds of cotton 7 cents per pound, $5.25, added to the value of the yarn, $3.75, is $9, the same value he started with, no surplus value has been created.

But our capitalist is fully alive to the situation.

He says, it is true that the past labor embodied in one day's labor-power is but 2 hours, yet that is no concern of mine.

What I bought was the use-value, and I am entitled to the use of the labor-power for such a length of time as will not exhaust more energy than can be restored during that portion of the 24 hours that it is not at work.

Here is the bone of contention between "capital and labor." "Capital" wants it to be exercised as long as possible, and "labor" is ever trying to shorten the working portion of the 24 hours.

However, our capitalist does get the use of the labor-power during 8 hours.

As one hour of labor creates the same value as another, every hour there is added $1 value to the cotton used up in producing the yarn.

The first two hours labor has created a value as great as the value of one day's labor-power.

And every 2 hours thereafter it creates a surplus-value equal to itself.

Hence in 8 hours the value added to the yarn is $8, or four times as great as the value of the day's labor-power.

At last the trick is turned.

Our capitalist paid out, for the raw material and means of production, $9, which has been converted into a commodity with a value of $15. Labor has created a surplus-value of $6, and money has been turned into capital.

If we now compare the two processes of producing value and of creating surplus-value, we see that the latter is nothing but the continuation of the former beyond a definite point.

We also see that the difference between labor, considered on the one hand as producing utilities, and on the other hand as creating values, resolves itself into a distinction between two aspects of the process of production.

The process of production considered as unity of the labor-process and the process of creating value, is production of commodities.

The process of production considered as the unity of the labor-process and the process of creating surplus-value, is the capitalist process of production, or capitalist production of commodities.

Chapter VIII. Constant Capital And Variable Capital.

The various factors of the labor process play different parts in forming the value of the product.

The laborer adds fresh value to the subject of his labor by expending upon it additional labor.

The values of the means of production are preserved, and present themselves afresh as constituent parts of the value of the products.

The values of the means of production pass over to the products, and are thus preserved.

This transfer takes place during the labor-process, it is brought about by labor; but how? The laborer does not perform two operations at once.

One in order to transfer the value of the cotton and part of the value of the spindle worn away, to the yarn, and another to add value to the cotton.

The two results, adding fresh value and preserving the former values, are brought about by one and the same operation. This is due to the twofold character of labor.

Now, if a use-value be effectually consumed in the production of a new use-value, the quantity of labor expended in the production of the consumed article forms a part of the labor necessary to produce the new use-value.

Hence it is in the character of concrete useful labor, applied with a definite aim, to produce some particular use-value that labor preserves values.

While it is in the character of abstract labor, applied with an aim to produce values, that labor creates surplus-values.

An interesting phenomenon here presents itself.

Suppose a machine to be worth $1,000 and to wear away in 1,000 days.

Then one-thousandth part of the value of the machine is daily transferred to the day's product.

At the same time, though with diminishing vitality, the machine as a whole continues to take part in the labor-process, while as an element of the formation of value it only enters by fractions.

On the other hand, the means of production may take part as a whole in the formation of value, while at the same time it enters into the labor-process only bit by bit.

If in the production of 100 pounds of yarn it is necessary that 15 pounds of cotton goes to waste, then 115 pounds of cotton is necessary for the production of 100 pounds of yarn and the 15 pounds of waste enters into the labor-process only bit by bit and it enters as a whole in the value of the yarn.

The same holds good for every kind of refuse not capable of forming a new and independent use-value.

The means of production transfers value to the new product only in so far, as during the labor-process, they lose value in the shape of their old use-value.

However useful a given kind of raw material, or a machine, or other means of production may be, though it may cost $4,000, or 500 days, it cannot, under any circumstances, add to the value of the product more than $4,000.

Its value is determined, not by the labor-process which it enters as a means of production, but by that out of which it has issued as a product.

The property which labor-power in action possesses of preserving value at the same time that it adds it, is a gift of nature, which costs the laborer nothing, but which is very advantageous to the capitalist, inasmuch as it preserves the existing value of the capital.

As regards the means of production, what is really consumed is their use-value, and the consumption of this use-value results in the product.

There is no consumption of their values; therefore, they are not reproduced.

We now see the different parts played by the various factors of the labor-process in the formation of the product's value.

That part of capital which represents the means of production raw material, machinery, auxiliary material, and instruments of labor — does not undergo any alteration in value.

I, therefore, call it the constant part of capital, or, more shortly, constant capital.

The part of capital represented by labor-power does undergo an alteration in value; it both produces the equivalent of its own value, and also a surplus-value, which may vary with circumstances.

The more productive the labor the greater the surplus-value created by it, and vise versa.

Chapter IX. The Rate Of Surplus-Value

Section 1. The degree of exploitation of labor.

The surplus-value generated in the process of production presents itself for our consideration as the amount by which the value of the product exceeds the value of its constituent elements.

The capital C is made up of two components, one c the sum of money laid out upon the means of production, and the other sum of money v expended upon the labor-power; C represents capital; c constant capital; and v variable capital; s surplus-value.

At first then, C=c+v; for example: if $500 is the capital advanced, its components may be such that $500=$410 constant plus $90 variable.

When the product is finished we get a commodity whose value=(c plus v) plus s, $410 plus v, $90, plus s $90, value of product, $590.

The original capital has changed from C $500 to C' $590.

We have seen how that portion of the constant capital which consists of the instruments of labor transfers to the product only a fraction of its value, while the remainder of that value continues to reside in those instruments.

To introduce it into the calculation would make no difference.

For instance, take our example:

Suppose this sum to consist of $312 value of raw material, $44 value of auxiliary material, and $54 value of the machinery worn away in the process, supposed that the value of the machinery employed is $1,054. If we reckon the remaining $1,000 as transferred to the product, we should also reckon it as advanced; then we would get $1,500 C and $1,590 C', still leaving $90 as the surplus.

The formula C=(c plus v) which we saw was transformed into C'=(c plus v) plus s, C becoming C'.

We know that the value of the constant capital is transferred to and reappears in the product.

The new value actually created in the process is not the same as the value of the product.

It is not as it would at first sight appear (c plus s), but (v plus s), $90 variable plus $90 surplus—not $590 but $180.

If there were branches of industry in which the capitalist could dispense with all the means of production made by previous labor, employing only labor-power and materials supplied by nature, there would be no constant capital to transfer to the product.

The component of the value of the product, that is the $410 in our example would be eliminated.

Our formula would then be, C'=(c plus v) plus s, or v plus s—$90 variable capital plus the $90 surplus, $180 the value of the product. The capital invested in labor-power is a definite quantity of materialized labor, a constant value, like the value of the labor-power purchased.

But in the process of production the place of the $90 is taken by the labor-power in action; dead labor is replaced by living labor, something stagnant by something flowing, a constant by a variable.

The result is the reproduction of v plus an increment of v.

From this point of view, then, of capitalist production, the whole process appears as the spontaneous variation of the original constant value which is transformed into labor power.

Both the process and its results appear to be oweing to this value.

If such expressions as $90 variable or "so much self-expanded value," appear contradictory, this is only because they bring to the surface a contradiction immanent in capitalist production.

At first sight it appears a strange proceeding to equate the constant capital to zero.

Yet this is what we do every day.

If we wish to calculate the amount of England's profit from the cotton industry, we first of all deduct the sum paid for cotton to the United States, India, Egypt, and other countries.

The value of the constant capital is put=0.

Given the new value produced=$180, subtract from it $90, the value of the variable capital, we have remaining $90 the amount of the surplus value.

The ratio of the surplus value to the variable capital is expressed by s/v.

In our example, this ratio is 90:90 or 100 per cent.

This relative increase in the value of variable capital, I call "the rate of surplus value."

The portion of the work-day that it requires to produce an equivalent of the labor embodied in the laborer — the time necessary to produce the subsistence of life, I call necessary labor-time, and the labor expended during that time I call necessary labor.

Necessary as regards the laborer, and necessary as regards the capitalist, because upon the existence of the laborer depends the existence of the capitalist.

During the second period of the process the laborer works, but his labor being no longer necessary he creates no value for himself.

He creates surplus-value for the capitalists, which has for them all the charms of a creation out of nothing.

This portion of the working day I name surplus labor-time, and to the labor expended during that time I give the name of surplus labor.

The rate of surplus-value is an exact expression of the degree of exploitation of labor-power by capital, or of the laborer by the capitalist.

The method of calculating the rate of surplus-value is as follows: Take the total value of the product, and put the constant capital equal to zero. If the amount of surplus-value be given deduct it from this remainder to find the variable capital, and if the variable capital be given deduct it from the remainder to find the surplus-value, then s/v gives us the ratio of the surplus-value to the variable capital.

Though the method is so simple, yet it may not be amiss, by means of an example, to exercise the reader in the application of the novel principle underlying it.

We will take the case of a spinning mill containing 10,000, mule spindles, spinning No. 2 yarn and producing one pound of yarn weekly per spindle.

Assume the waste to be 6 per cent and 10,600 pounds of cotton are consumed weekly, at a price of 6 cents per pound, which gives us $636 as the cost of raw material.

The 10,000 spindles, motive power, and all accessories we set at $50,000, the wear and tear of which we put at $100 per week, rent of building $80 a week, coal, gas, oil and auxiliary materials—$84 a week. As the total, of constant capital, we have $636, $100, $80, $84, or $900. We will assume the variable capital to be $300 a week. The price of yarn we will put at 21 cents per pound or a total of $1200. The surplus-value is, therefore, $1200 less $900 constant capital and less the $300 variable or $900.

Put the constant capital at zero, there remains $1200 as the amount of value created weekly. The rate of surplus value is, then, as $300 variable is to $900 surplus, or 300 per cent. In a working day of eight hours the result is necessary-labor two hours, surplus-labor six hours.

Chapter X. The Working-Day

The Limits of the Working Day

We started with the supposition that labor-power is bought and sold at its value.

Its value, like that of all other commodities, is determined by the working time necessary for its production.

If the production of the average daily means of subsistence of the laborer takes up six hours he must work, on the average, six hours every day to produce his daily labor-power, or to reproduce the value received as the result of its sale.

The necessary part of his working-day amounts to six hours, and is, other things being equal, a given quantity.

But with this, the extent of the working-day itself is not given.

To illustrate we will make a line A B representing the necessary working time—say six hours. If the working time be prolonged one, three or six hours beyond B, we have three other lines:

A —-- -- --- — B — C working-day I.
A — — — — — — B — — — C working-day II.
A — B — — — — --- C working-day III.

Representing three different working-days of 7, 9 and 12 hours.

The extension BC of the line AB represents the length of the surplus labor.

As the working-day is AB plus BC, or AC, it varies with the variable quantity BC.

Since AB is constant, the ratio of BC to AB can always be calculated.

In working-day I it is one-sixth; in working-day II it is three-sixths; in working-day III it is six-sixths of AB.

Since, further, the ratio surplus-working-time to necessary working-time determines the rate of surplus-value, the latter is given by the ratio of BC to AB.

It amounts in the three different working-days, respectively, to 16 2/3, 50 and 100 per cent.

On the other hand, the rate of surplus alone would not give us the extent of the working-day.

If this rate, for example, were 100 percent, the working-day might be 8, 10, 12 or more hours.

It would indicate that the two constituent parts of the working-day, necessary-labor and surplus labor-time, were equal in extent, but not how long each of these two constituent parts was.

The working-day is thus not a constant, but a variable, quantity.

One of its parts, certainly, is determined by the working-time required for the reproduction of the labor-power or the laborer himself.

But its total amount varies with the duration of the surplus-labor.

The working-day is, therefore, determinable, but is, considered by itself, indeterminate.

Although the working-day is not a fixed, but a fluent quantity, it can, on the other hand, only vary within certain limits.

The minimum limit is, however, not determinable.

Of course, if we make the extension line BC or the surplus-labor=0, we have a minimum limit; that is, the part of the day which the laborer must work for his own maintenance.

On the basis of capitalist production, however, this necessary labor can form a part only of the working-day; the working-day itself can never be reduced to this minimum.

On the other hand, the working-day has a maximum limit. It cannot be prolonged beyond a certain point.

This maximum limit is conditioned by two things. First, by the physical bounds of labor-power—within the 24 hours of the natural day a man can expend only a definite quantity of this vital force.

During part of the day this force must rest, sleep; during another part the man has to satisfy other purely physical needs – to feed, wash and clothe himself.

Besides these purely physical limits, the extension of the working-day encounter moral ones.

The laborer needs time to satisfy his intellectual and social wants, the extent and number of which are conditioned by the general state of social advancement.

The variations of the working-day fluctuates, therefore, within physical and social bonds.

But both these limiting conditions are of a very elastic nature, and allowing the greatest latitude.

So we find working-days of 8, 10, 12, 14, 16, 18 hours – that is, of the most different lengths

The capitalist has bought the labor-power at its day-rate.

To him its use-value belongs during one working-day.

He has thus acquired the right to make the laborer work for him during one day.

But, what is a working-day? At all events less than a natural day.

By how much? The capitalist has his own views of this ultimate limit, the necessary limit of the working-day.

As capitalist, he is only capital personified. His soul is the soul of capital.

But capital has one single life impulse – the tendency to create capital and surplus-value, to make its constant factor, the means of production, absorb the greatest possible amount of surplus-labor.

Capital is dead labor, that, vampire-like, only lives by sucking living labor, and lives the more the more labor it sucks.

The time the laborer works is the time during which the capitalist consumes the labor-power he has purchased from him.

If the labor consumes his disposable time for himself, he robs the capitalist.

The capitalist then takes his stand on the law of the exchange of commodities.

He, like all other buyers, seeks to get the greatest possible benefit out of the use-value of his commodity.

Suddenly the voice of the laborer, which has been stiffled in the storm and stress of the process of production, rises:

The commodity that I have sold to you differs from the crowd of other commodities, in that its use-value creates value, and a value greater than its own.

That is why you bought it.

That which on your side appears a spontaneous expansion of capital, is on mine extra expenditure of labor-power.

You and I know on the market only one law — that of the exchange of commodities.

And the consumption of the commodity belongs not to the seller who parts with it, but to the buyer who acquires it.

To you, therefore, belongs the use-value of my daily labor-power.

But by means of the price you pay for it each day I must be able to reproduce it daily; and sell it again.

Apart from natural exhaustion through age, etc., I must be able on the morrow to work with the same normal amount of force, health and freshness as today.

You preach to me constantly the gospel of "saving" and "abstinence." Good! I will, like a sensible, saving owner, husband my sole wealth, labor-power, and abstain from all foolish waste of it.

I will each day spend, set in motion, put into action, only as much of it as is compatible with its normal duration and healthy development.

By an unlimited extension of the working-day, you may in one day use up a quantity of labor-power greater than I can restore in three.

What you gain in labor I lose in substance.

The use of my labor-power and the spoiliation of it are quite different things.

If the average working life of a laborer is 30 years, the value of my labor-power, per day, which you pay me for is 1-365th multiplied by 30, or 1-10950th of its total value.

But if you consume it in 10 years, you pay me daily 1-10950th instead of 1-3650th of its total value; that is, one-third of its daily value, and you rob me, therefore, every day of two-thirds of the value of my commodity.

You pay me for I day's labor-power, whilst you use that of 3.

This is against our contract and the law of exchanges.

I demand, therefore, a working-day of normal length, and I demand it without any appeal to your heart, for in money matters sentiment is out of place.

You may be a model citizen, perhaps a member of the Society for the Prevention of Cruelty to Animals, and in the Order of Sanctity to boot, but the thing that you represent face to face with me has no heart in its breast.

That which seems to throb there is my own heart-beating.

I demand the normal working-day, because I, like every other seller, demand the value of my commodity.

NOTE—During the great strike of the London builders, 1860-61, for the reduction of the working-day to 9 hours, their committee published a manifesto that contained, to the same extent, the plea of our worker.

The manifesto alludes, not without irony, to the fact that the greatest profit-monger among the building masters, a certain M. Petro, was in the Order of Sanctity.

We see then that, apart from extremely elastic bounds, the nature of the exchange of commodities itself imposes no limit to the working-day, no limit to the surplus-labor.

The capitalist maintains his right as purchaser when he tries to make the working-day as long as possible, and to make when possible two working-days out of one.

On the other hand, the peculiar nature of the commodity sold implies a limit to its consumption by the purchaser, and the laborer maintains his right as seller when he wishes to reduce the working-day to one of definite normal duration.

There is here, therefore, an antimony, right against right, both equally bearing the seal of the law of exchanges.

Between equal rights force decides.

Hence is it that, in the history of capitalist production, the determination of what is a working-day presents itself as a struggle— a struggle between collective capital, that is, the capitalist class, and collective labor, that is the working class.

The concept of relative surplus-value.

That portion of the working-day which merely produces an equivalent paid by the capitalist for his labor-power has, up to this point, been treated by us as a constant magnitude; and such in fact it is, under given conditions of production and at a given stage in the economical development of society.

Beyond this, his necessary labor-time, the laborer, we saw, could continue to work for 2, 3, 4, 6, etc., hours.

The sate of surplus-value and the length of the working-day depended on the magnitude of this prolongation.

Though the necessary labor-time was constant, we saw, on the other hand, that the total working-day was variable.

Now, suppose we have a working-day whose length, and whose apportionment between necessary labor and surplus-labor are given.

Let the whole line, A C, A_etc, represent, for example, a working-day of 12 hours; the portion of a 10 hours of necessary labor, and the portion b c 2 hours of surplus-labor.

How now can the production of surplus-value be increased — that is, how can the surplus-labor be prolonged, without, or independently of, any prolongation of A C?

Although the length of A C is given, B C appears to be capable of prolongation, if not by extension beyond its end C, which is also the end of the working-day A C, yet at all events, by pushing back its starting starting point b in the direction of A.

Assume that B' — B in the line of a B' B C is equal to half of B C, B'..B...C, or to one hour's labor-time.

If now in A C, the working-day of 12 hours, we move the point B to B', B C becomes B' C; the surplus-labor increases by one-half, from 2 hours to 3 hours, although the working-day remains, as before, 12 hours.

This extension of the surplus labor-time from 2 hours to 3 hours is, however, evidently impossible without a simultaneous contraction of the necessary labor-time from A B into A B', from 10 hours to 9 hours.

The prolongation of the surplus-labor would correspond to shortening of the necessary labor; or a portion of the labor-time previously consumed, in reality, for the laborer's own benefit, would be converted into labor-time for the benefit of the capitalist.

There would be an alteration, not in the length of the working-day, but in its division into necessary labor-time and surplus labor-time.

On the other hand, it is evident that the duration of the surplus-labor is given, when the length of the working-day and the value of labor-power are given.

The value of labor-power, that is the labor-time requisite to produce labor-power, determines the labor-time necessary for the reproduction of that value.

If in one working-hour be embodied 12 cents, and the value of a day's labor-power be $1.20, the laborer must work 10 hours a day in order to replace the value paid by capital for his labor-power, or to produce an equivalent for the value of his daily necessary means of subsistence.

Given the value of these means of subsistence, the value of his labor-power is given; and, given the value of his labor-power, the duration of his necessary labor-time is given.

The duration of the surplus-labor, however, is arrived at by subtracting the necessary labor-time from the total working-day.

Ten hours subtracted from 12 leaves 2; and it is not easy to see how, under the given conditions, the surplus-labor can possibly be prolonged beyond 2 hours.

No doubt the capitalist can, instead of $1.20, pay the laborer $1.08 or even less.

For the reproduction of this value 9 hours would suffice; and consequently 3 hours of surplus-labor, instead of 2, would accrue to the capitalist, and the surplus-value would rise from 24 cents to 36 cents.

This result, however, would be obtained only by lowering the wages of the laborer below the value of his labor-power.

With the $1.08 which he produced in 9 hours, he commands one-tenth less of the necessaries of life than before, and consequently the proper reproduction of his labor-power is crippled.

This is where many stop in their investigation of the labor problem.

In consequence of which we find the calamity howler and pseudo-socialists on soap boxes haranguing the passersby.

Telling the workers "that their wages, and also the standard of living is continually falling, and that, unless they join the ranks to which the 'howler' belongs, the working men of America will soon sink to the level of the Asiatic laborer."

And worse still is their egregious error "that the working men refrain from joining their ranks on account of the gross ignorance on the part of the working men. "

The fact of the matter is, that the working men have too high an intelligence to be caught by such chaff.

They know that their wages have continually raised since 1850, and that the standard of living is much higher than it was in the past.

The conditions stated in a previous chapter, also apply here:

The conversion of money into capital has to be explained on the basis of the laws that regulate the exchange of commodities, in such a way that the starting-point is the exchange of equivalents. The capitalist must buy his commodities at their value and sell them at their value—this includes the commodity, labor-power.

What must take place in order that we may, without in any way violating the law, as above laid down, shorten the necessary labor-time? Increase the productiveness of labor.

The surplus-value produced by prolongation of the working-day I call absolute surplus-value.

On the other hand, the surplus-value arising from the curtailment of the necessary labor-time, and from the corresponding alteration in the respective lengths of the two components of the working-day, I call relative surplus-value.

In order to effect a fall in the value of labor-power, the increase in the productiveness of labor must seize upon those branches of industry whose products determine the value of labor power, and consequently either belong to the class of customary means of subsistence, or are capable of supplying the place of those means.

But the value of a commodity is determined not only by the quantity of labor which the laborer bestows upon that commodity, but also by the labor contained in the means of production.

For instance, the value of a pair of boots depends, not only on the cobbler's labor, but also on the value of the leather, wax, thread, etc.

Hence a fall in the value of labor-power is also brought about by an increase in the productiveness of labor, and by a corresponding cheapening of commodities in those industries which supply the instruments of labor and the raw material, that form the elements of the constant capital required for producing the necessaries of life.

In 1850 the normal working-day was 10 hours, and the average yearly wage was $180.

The necessary labor was four and eight-tenths hours, and surplus-value five and two-tenths hours.

Since 1850 the productiveness of labor has increased forty-fold.

Had the standard of living remained constant, the necessary labor would now be only one-quarter of an hour. But all our wants, both physical and mental, have greatly increased, and, while we still have many wants unsatisfied, those that are satisfied are eight-fold greater than those of 1850.

Hence, the necessary labor today is represented by two hours.

Our working-day has also been reduced to eight hours. So by this it is plainly seen that the statements of our "calamity howler" is false, for both wages and the standard of living have greatly increased.

But when we consider the ratio between necessary labor and surplus-value, we find that the working man has got the "little end of the stick."

For now the ratio is: two hours necessary labor and six hours surplus-value.

Thus, while the wages have risen from $180 to $388 a year, and the standard of living increased eight-fold, by the increased productiveness of labor, this increased productiveness of labor has not been of as great a benefit to the laborer as to the capitalist.

The great social discontent arises out of the conditions that make for human progress.

The physical betterment must of necessity precede the higher intellectual development.

The better food, clothing and shelter gives a stronger and more highly developed physical organism, to supply energy to a more finely developed and intensified brain.

Being surrounded by more beautiful buildings, parks, art galleries, conservatories of music, boulevards and gardens, the human mind is stimulated, and our desires are greatly increased.

It is not that our conditions are getting worse, as the "calamity howler" would make us believe, but that, by our present system of production—the capitalist system—our progress is greatly retarded.

The intelligent wage-worker recognizes that our capitalist system of production was a necessary condition to the progress of the human race, in that it socialized the industries, brought about labor-saving machinery, and the scientific division of labor, which so greatly increased its productiveness.

When each individual produced by and for himself, and exchanged the product of his labor directly with one other person, his instincts were atomic, and his thoughts were always individual, or anarchistic. This is shown by his cry of individual liberty, freedom, etc.

Surrounded only by primitive conditions his horizon of thought was very limited.

But with the socialization of industry it is quite different.

Like all other systems, the present one holds the germ of its own destruction.

By the bringing together a large number of workers in one factory, specializing their labor, the social instinct is bred.

For instance, where one man makes a mold, another pours the iron, another conveys it to the machine, where another bores it out — where one man cuts the bars, another turns up the ends — and another presses the car wheels on the axle, and so on till they are placed under a car.

No one of these can think of his own action except by associating the action of all the others, whose actions were applied for the same end — that of making a car.

Thus the horizon of his thoughts gains scope until he finds that the hat-maker, tailor, weaver, potato digger, in short every other worker is but a link in the chain of production, and that every person is dependent upon every other person.

He realizes that, just as each cell of his body is an integral part of his organism, every individual member is an integral part of the organism society.

Hence, his every effort is to so conduct himself that all his actions will be for the social good, as he realizes that his highest self-interest is to work for a more stable and better social fabric.

As he learns that a healthy body requires that all its members should be in a healthy condition, that if one member has a fungus or parasitic growth that it draws its substance from, and impoverishes, all the rest of the body, and prevents its development.

That when any member becomes rudimentary, and useless, that the sooner it is gone the better it is for the rest of the body.

So with our body social, every member must be in a healthy condition — economically — to have a stable and healthy society.

We have reached that stage in our economic development where all production is social, and the only thing compatible with social production would be social distribution.

Therefore the capitalist has become a parasite sucking surplus-value from the working class without performing any useful service to society.

And the sooner we lop off (not the man, but the function of) the capitalist the better for the welfare of the body politic.

www.ingramcontent.com/pod-product-compliance
Lightning Source LLC
Chambersburg PA
CBHW060857280326
41934CB00007B/1090